CREATE YOUR WRITER PLATFORM

CREATE YOUR WRITER PLATFORM

The Key to Building an Audience, Selling More Books, and Finding Success as an Author

WRITER'S DIGEST
BOOKS

WritersDigest.com
Cincinnati, Ohio

Chuck Sambuchino

For more resources for writers, visit www.writersdigest.com/books.

To receive a free weekly e-mail newsletter delivering tips and updates about writing and about Writer's Digest products, register directly at www.writersdigest.com/enews.

16 15 14 13   5 4 3 2

Distributed in Canada by Fraser Direct
100 Armstrong Avenue
Georgetown, Ontario, Canada L7G 5S4
Tel: (905) 877-4411

Distributed in the U.K. and Europe by F&W Media International
Brunel House, Newton Abbot, Devon, TQ12 4PU, England
Tel: (+44) 1626-323200, Fax: (+44) 1626-323319
E-mail: enquiries@fwmedia.com

Distributed in Australia by Capricorn Link
P.O. Box 704, Windsor, NSW 2756 Australia
Tel: (02) 4577-3555

Edited by Rachel Scheller
Designed by Claudean Wheeler
Cover illustrations by eve/Fotolia.com
Production coordinated by Debbie Thomas

DEDICATION

To every writer who struggles toward a goal
and hopes tomorrow will bring something great.
You are not alone. This book is for you.

ACKNOWLEDGMENTS

The first person to thank is my wife, Bre, for all her love and encouragement. She is my rock and my light.

Next I want to thank all those who had a hand in making this book a reality. My agent, Sorche Fairbank, is a wonderful guide for all my projects. My editor, Rachel Scheller (who sits right next to me at work), did a great job making this book better. I want to thank Phil Sexton, publisher of Writer's Digest, for helping me get this book off the ground, as well as designer Claudean Wheeler for her great cover. Wise publishing professionals Brian A. Klems, Alexis Grant, Patricia V. Davis, Ricki Schultz, and Mare Swallow all helped me shape chapters as I went along. Their advice was invaluable, and I am very grateful. Publishing wise man Robert Brewer contributed several sidebars to the guide. Thank you, Robert.

I owe a great debt of gratitude to all the literary agents who contributed quotes and all the authors who participated in interviews. The agents who helped me were Stephany Evans, Meredith Barnes (now a publicist), Gina Panettieri, Verna Dreisbach, Roseanne Wells, Alyssa Reuben, John Willig, Shawna Morey, Bernadette Baker-Baughman, and Laurie Abkemeier. Publicists and editors who chimed in and deserve a shout-out include Hector DeJean, Beth Gissinger, and Lisa Laing. Lastly, to all the case study authors who took so much time to explain their routes to success, I say thank you. Everyone reading this guide should go out and buy their books. These are authors who love helping other authors.

To all the other writers and publishing pros who contributed quotes or answered my questions, I am in debt to you.

Table of Contents

Author Case Studies

Final Thoughts

Introduction

As a teacher of writing and publishing, I speak at a dozen writers conferences a year. At those conferences, if I had to pick the question I'm asked most frequently, it would probably be: "How do all the drastic changes to the publishing industry affect aspiring writers?"

Before I answer, let's examine the question itself. Writers are essentially asking, "Because the marketplace is changing, and I've been told it's more difficult to be an author today than it was ten or twenty years ago, how can I best be prepared as a writer?" All kinds of things are at play in this question: How can we work smarter? How can we deal with industry evolution? How can we make our writing dreams come true?

You're starting to see that this is a *huge* question—but, in my opinion, a very necessary one. It's necessary because the fears behind it are absolutely justified: It is more difficult to be a successful writer now than in decades past. The ease of publishing e-books online means that more books are created now than ever before. That means more competition for you—not to mention fewer brick-and-mortar bookstores, where buyers can see your work. And sure, people are reading a lot these days, as many news articles have pointed out—but that doesn't necessarily mean they're *buying books*, which is what matters most to authors.

In years past, my stock answer to this question was always, "Just create the best book you can." In other words, I would encourage writers to simply *write*, and let a publishing house worry about how best to distribute their work and maximize e-book potential in a changing industry. But now my answer has changed. Today, when presented with this huge question, my reply is, "First, just write the best book you can. Second, take steps to build your writer platform."

How did a strange term like *platform* find its way into my answer? Let's rewind for a moment.

Because of the gravitation toward free content online, industry layoffs (hitting editors and publicists the hardest) and a slew of other factors, publishers are taking fewer chances with new writers because, simply put, their budgets can't support it. To combat dwindling sales numbers, publishers have turned to defensive tactics, such as printing fewer copies of books. But the other thing they've begun to do to protect themselves—and the reason you're holding this book—is that they've also started to take a close look at each writer's platform. With so many books in the marketplace and few publicists to help promote, the burden now lies upon the author to make sure copies of his or her book fly off bookshelves. In other words, the pressure is on for writers to act as their own publicists and chief marketers—though few can do this successfully.

> "Now, authors need more than good book ideas; they must be perceived by publishers as being entrepreneurial, promotion-minded, and willing to aggressively market their books. To make those determinations, publishers look to an author's platform."
> —RICK FRISHMAN AND ROBYN FREEDMAN SPIZMAN, *from their book,* Author 101: Bestselling Book Proposals

Having an effective writer platform has never been more important than it is right now. It's because a writer platform is one of the best tools (if not the *only* tool) a writer can use to personally combat publishing challenges. Yes, it's hard to get a book published and make sure it sells once it's out there—so what's a writer to do? The first thing you can

CREATE YOUR WRITER PLATFORM

do is simply get back to basics. If you write a damn good book, people will pay it mind, sure. But if that book is nonfiction, a damn good book won't cut it. You need to prove that people will buy it by showing a comprehensive ability to market yourself through different channels such as social networking sites and traditional media. If you can't do that, a traditional publisher won't even consider your idea. I'll repeat that for emphasis: If you don't have a proven ability to promote your work and sell books, editors won't even consider your idea, no matter how clever or timely it may be.

If you want to write a nonfiction book, you *must* have a platform in order to get editors to consider your work. If you're writing fiction or memoir, a platform isn't mandatory, but it will certainly help your chances (especially with memoir)—and it translates to more book sales and money for you once your title is released. And with the way things are trending, who knows? In five or ten years, a writer platform may be mandatory for *any* book. That's why it's so vital to start thinking about platform *now*, and that's the reason why I sat down to write this book. I wanted to create a guide for all the hardworking writers out there who want a say in their own destinies. This book is for scribes who want to do everything they can to invest in their work and guarantee themselves success. It is not for a writer who puts his first chapter on a brand new website and sits back, wondering why editors aren't banging down the door with a six-figure offer.

The instruction of *Create Your Writer Platform* is three-fold. The first thing you will learn, in detail, is what *platform* means, why it's important, and how utilizing broad principles will help you succeed no matter what specific path you choose. The second section of this book illuminates the nuts-and-bolts steps of how you can build up your own platform through any number of means, be that public speaking or social media or creating a blog. In the final portion, you can read case studies of those who have built their platforms from the ground up— to hear expertise from a variety of sources and journeys.

The third section of this book—author interviews—will be key. I quickly realized that although I've had success in platform building, my knowledge is still limited, and I could only share examples about *my* journey in *my* field of writing/publishing. I collected a lot of outside opinions and stories so you can get a sense of the many possible paths that lead to platform. I reached out to literary agents and successful writers with questions, and most of them responded, because they understand as well as I do how incredibly crucial this subject is in today's writing world.

This is not a book about advertising, nor a guide explaining how to get a review in the *New York Times* for your book that's already out. (That's *publicity*, not platform. You will soon learn how they are connected yet quite different.) This is not a book for those who want to work as little as possible and who complain about how no one is buying their stuff. This is a serious guide for serious writers who want to grow their visibility and explore new ways to become a successful author. This is a resource for those who realize that selling a book is not about blatant self-promotion. It's about building relationships one channel and one plank at a time through platform—be those channels and planks online or personal. Platform is the future ... so let's get started.

"Platform is your multifaceted effort to put yourself 'out there' in a variety of ways as a blogger, speaker, self-promoter, teacher, impresario, host, critic, media schmoozer, networker. If you have a traditional publisher, they will give you and your book some attention for a limited amount of time. Then, more than ever, it's up to you to get the word out on your book and to come up with new, fresh ideas that keep you and your book, or your future book, in the minds of editors, readers, reviewers, audience members, and opinion leaders."
—**ETHAN GILSDORF**, *freelancer for national magazines/ blogs and author of the memoir* Fantasy Freaks and Gaming Geeks

THE PRINCIPLES OF PLATFORM

CHAPTER 1
What *Is* Platform?

Platform, simply put, is your *visibility as an author*.

It's your personal ability to sell books right this instant. It is not "what you would be willing to do," but rather "what you can do and what you bring to the table *right now*." Better yet, I've always thought of platform like this: When you speak, who's listening? In other words, when you have something to say, what legitimate channels exist for you to release your message to audiences who will consider buying your books/services?

If you found yourself staring off into space just now, realizing that you have virtually no platform, fear not. Having no platform is expected. It's normal. To get one requires a concerted effort to reach out to groups and individuals with the goal of building a following. If you haven't done that yet, you're starting from zero—but that's quite all right. Everyone does.

The definition of platform, broken down, is your personal ability to sell books through:

1. Who you are
2. The personal and professional connections you have
3. Any media outlets (including blogs and social networks) that you can utilize to sell books

The best platform is, of course, fame. That's why it seems like every celebrity is writing a memoir or children's picture book these days. Sure, the books may not be that good, but because of the celebrity's public reach and notoriety, the books are guaranteed to sell well—and that's why publishers are interested. Celebrities have platform, plain and simple, and that *reach* translates to money and success.

To understand platform, let's imagine a "Platform Scale" that goes from zero to one hundred, the former being absolutely no platform and the latter being the best platform imaginable. Who would be at one hundred? For my money, it's Oprah. Think of all the ways she is visible—huge magazine, top-ranking TV show (reruns now), popular radio programs, a brand of authority and expertise, high-profile charity endeavors, and much more. Everyone knows who she is, and most everyone trusts her for advice on products to buy. Not only is she plugged into so many outlets where people can see and hear her, but these outlets are extremely big, and she has developed a trustworthy brand. She has a perfect platform, and that's why inclusion in her book club has generated success for authors.

Now let's imagine someone whose platform is at zero. This, in my mind, would be a writer who never leaves the house, doesn't like meeting new people (even on the phone), and still works on a Word Processor because he doesn't own a computer. This person possesses absolutely no ability to do any self-marketing. Hopefully this is not you, and you have at least some reach into various communities and are willing to work hard to build more.

"The two highest levels of influence are achieved when 1) people follow you because of what you've done for them, and 2) people follow you because of who you are. In other words, the highest levels of influence are reached when generosity and trustworthiness surround your behavior."

—DALE CARNEGIE *and the authors of* How to Win Friends & Influence People in the Digital Age

In this guide, we will discuss the nitty-gritty building blocks of a platform. I want to delve into all the channels a writer has to reach his audience and establish connections. In my opinion, the most common building blocks of a platform include the following:

1. A website and/or blog with a large readership
2. An e-newsletter and/or mailing list with a large number of subscribers/recipients
3. Article/column writing (or correspondent involvement) for the media—preferably for larger outlets and outlets within the writer's specialty
4. Guest contributions to successful websites, blogs, and periodicals
5. A track record of strong past book sales[1]
6. Individuals of influence that you know—personal contacts (organizational, media, celebrity, relatives) who can help you market at no cost to yourself, whether through blurbs, promotion, or other means
7. Public speaking appearances—the bigger, the better
8. An impressive social media presence (Twitter, Facebook, and the like)
9. Membership in organizations that support the successes of their own
10. Recurring media appearances and interviews—in print, on the radio, on TV, or online

Not all of these methods will be of interest/relevance to you. As you learn more about how to find success in each one, some will jump out as practical and feasible, while others will not. My advice is to choose a few and dive in deep—and don't be afraid to concede failure in one area, then shift gears and plunge into something else. It's better to show impressive success in some areas than minimal success in all.

---

[1] Simply having books to your name does not give you a platform. The titles in question must have performed well in the marketplace. Most self-published books do not constitute sizeable platform avenues, as most do not sell thousands of copies. A book would have to take off in sales and/or downloads (even if it's free) in order to help your visibility and get your brand moving forward.

Lastly, know that building a platform takes time. Strive for something real—strong channels that will help you sell. Simply being on Twitter and having a website does not mean you have a platform. Those are just the first steps.

"WHAT IS PLATFORM?"

"I have a simple formula for platform: Authority + Network = Platform. *Authority* to speak on a subject (self-help, spirituality, business, economics, etc.) is basically why you are the best person to write this book. And *Network* is whom you know that will buy the book. These two main elements play into each other, and having one helps the other. Platform is literally what you can stand on—what supports you as an author."

—**ROSEANNE WELLS** *(Marianne Strong Literary Agency)*

"A platform is the people who know and love you and your writing now, as opposed to all those hypothetical people that will know you once your book is bought and you get motivated to do all of that social media stuff. They're the built-in audience that you bring to the table along with your book idea—because the publisher will be buying both."

—**MEREDITH BARNES** *(formerly of Lowenstein Associates, Inc.)*

"A platform showcases the experiences you've had that qualify you as an expert in your field, which advocate your successes and serve as a vehicle for your publicity."

—**BERNADETTE BAKER-BAUGHMAN** *(Victoria Sanders & Associates)*

"I find that the three questions I get asked about a writer's platform from a potential publisher are: What is their website traffic? How many Twitter followers do they have? And how many Facebook fans do they have? Of course, any big publicity hits (e.g., an appearance on a morning show, an article in a prominent magazine), or speaking engagements help—but those three components (Facebook, Twitter, personal blog/website), are key indicators of a person's platform and should be built up as much as possible."

—ALYSSA REUBEN (*Paradigm Literary*)

"Writer platform is comparable to the listenership of a specific radio station or the viewership of a particular television program."

—SHAWNA MOREY (*Folio Literary Management*)

"I define a writer's platform as all the methods the author has of reaching the buyer, whether it's the end consumer book buyer or the bookstore owner or chain buyer. Consider your platform your tool to discoverability for your book, so that potential readers can find you."

—GINA PANETTIERI (*Talcott Notch Literary Services*)

"The term *platform* describes the ways you reach out to people—such as a campus radio show, lecture tour, or popular blog. The term also refers to people interested in what you write, as if they allowed you to stand on their shoulders, elevating you as you raise your literary voice. Those people include others you've drawn into your orbit by networking. A strong platform describes the ways in which a writer is visible or connected to a community of potential or actual readers."

—REGINA BROOKS (*Serendipity Literary Agency*)

CHAPTER 2

THE NECESSITY OF PLATFORM

"Here's the secret: You have to be more than a writer. You have to be an expert on a topic or a creator or an entrepreneur or a salesman—or maybe a combination of several of those. Too many could-be authors shun the idea of self-promotion, saying they just want to write. Which is fine—if you're not hoping to make any money off your books (in which case no publisher would buy them). If you want this to be your job, if you want writing to support you, you have to be more than a writer."

—**ALEXIS GRANT**, *social media and platform coach*

You picked up this book because of one simple fact: More books are getting published now than before and fewer publicists are around to get the word out. It's a crowded marketplace—and competition for attention will only get tougher. The shift toward e-books and ease in digital publishing means that anybody can publish anything and increase market competition even further.

When I sit down with self-published authors and ask them what infrastructure they have in place to market their work, if their first response is, "The book is available on Amazon," I know they're in trouble. Do you know how many books are available on Amazon? More than five million, last I checked. Even within a specific category such as psychology, you're still up against at least five thousand titles. That's a *lot* of competition, and more competition makes it hard for people to locate your work and buy it.

We've just touched upon the key—having readers *find* your book. Even if your book provides dynamite information and has a great design with good reviews, if readers can't find it and don't know it exists, then you're stuck at square one. If you want a major publisher to pay you and then release your book, you must be your own marketing department—and you must be effective.

The necessity and value of a platform is a somewhat touchy subject. I've met hundreds of writers who are wonderful, intelligent people with excellent book ideas. Then I ask them about their platform, and they go blank. When I explain that their book idea is of little to no value without an accompanying platform, their expression goes from blank to angry. "I don't understand," they'll say. "I've taken the time to conceive and compose a very worthwhile, helpful book. This has taken years of my time. Why can't the publisher distribute, market, and publicize the work? Isn't that what they're there for?"

Well, not exactly. But, to be clear, there are certainly things that a publisher *will* do for you in today's marketplace:

- **PUBLISHERS WILL EDIT THE WORK.** Their job is to transform your text or manuscript from good to great, and/or from great to amazing.
- **PUBLISHERS WILL DESIGN THE BOOK AND ITS COVER.** This is very important. Despite what the old adage says, books are absolutely judged by their front and back covers.

- **PUBLISHERS WILL DISTRIBUTE THE BOOK.** They should at least have it available in major bookstores (Barnes & Noble, Books-A-Million) as well as on the most highly-trafficked book-buying websites, such as Amazon and bn.com. If possible, they will also get it into specialty shops, such as Michaels, Lowes, or Babies "R" Us.
- **PUBLISHERS WILL PAY YOU.** Traditional publishers pay authors—either a flat fee or an advance against royalties. If you inked the deal thanks to an agent, she is entitled to roughly 15 percent of your earnings for her efforts.

"We may love a project, but it's always going to come down to who will buy it. A lot of blood, sweat, moolah, and tears go into publishing and selling a book—so it's no surprise that publishers would want to hedge their bets, as we would if the shoe were on the other foot. An author might find it useful to put themselves in the publisher's place and address the question, 'If I were going to publish this myself (as virtually anyone can do now), how would I reach readers who will pull out their wallets for this book?' It's a good exercise. Then they'd begin to see that unless they build it, and raise a flag on it, very few would even know it's there, let alone come."

—STEPHANY EVANS, *co-founding literary agent, FinePrint Literary Management*

Publishers definitely bring important aspects to the table. That's the good news. The bad news is that the old perceived method of books solely being marketed by publicists is no longer the case. The best you can hope for now is that a publicist will assist you in marketing a book. If you get that much, consider it a victory. But many books—including an overwhelming majority of low-print-run titles in the marketplace released by smaller publishing houses—will rely on the marketing of the author alone. Sure, word of mouth can help; people in the media may read it and write about it—but neither of those is guaranteed.

Only the absolute top-tier authors, such as James Patterson and Stephenie Meyer, have no need to market their work because a professional takes care of all their marketing needs. For everyone else—especially nonfiction, memoir, and all self-published scribes—platform and marketing are of the utmost importance. And here's an extremely vital thing to note: *The necessity of platform is not going away.* If you're sitting around waiting for the book industry to hire more staff to do work for you while also waiting for eight-track tapes to become popular again, you will get left behind. "Platform will only become more and more important," says Beth Gissinger, digital marketing director for F+W Media. "As the industry continues to move digitally, online platform will become the biggest driver."

If you haven't noticed, publishing companies have laid off an alarming percentage of staff in the past five years. The most heavily affected groups are editors and publicists. Those who remain are overworked. Publicists just don't have time to market all their books to the fullest. Not only that, but the success of publicists relies on connections and the people they know. So even if a publicist has the time and energy to put behind your campaign, she must also have the appropriate knowledge and connections for your book's genre—say, woodworking markets, for example—in order to be as effective as you would hope.

"Getting a book published does not equate to readership. You must cultivate a readership every day of your life, and start today. Audience development doesn't happen overnight (or even in six months or a year)—and it's a process that continues for as long as you want to have a readership. It shouldn't be delayed, postponed, or discounted for one minute."

These two big reasons are why, over the past ten years, there has been a huge and monumental shift toward only signing nonfiction authors who have built-in readerships. An author with a platform not only has the ability to communicate with her target audience immediately (and sell books), but also has an expertise regarding the target market itself and understands/knows the most logical media outlets that would be interested in her book. It's a win on all levels for a publisher if the author is a smart and connected marketer.

If you're writing nonfiction—and therefore composing a book proposal as your major selling tool—there are three major questions to answer in your proposal:

1. What is your book and why is it unique?
2. What is your book's place in the market?
3. Why are you the best person to write this book?

Now, out of those three main questions, which would you consider to be the most important? The logical choice would be #1, but the correct answer is actually #3—because within that third question is the *inspection of your platform*. If you don't have a platform and you lack the ability to successfully self-market your work to audiences who potentially will buy it, then, as Metallica once said, "nothing else matters." It's that simple. Think about what platform is—it's *visibility*. So a book without a platform is just the opposite: invisible. And why would a publisher spend tens of thousands of dollars on a book that no one can find just to lose money? They won't!

BOOK PROPOSALS

A book proposal is a business plan that explains all the details of a nonfiction book. If you're writing a work of fiction (novel, screenplay, picture book) or memoir, the first all-important step is to simply *finish* the work, because agents and editors will consider it for publication based primarily on how good the writing is.

On the other hand, when you have a nonfiction project of any kind, you do *not* need to finish the book to sell it. In fact, even if you're feeling ambitious and knock out the entire text, finishing the book will not help you sell it because all an editor really needs to see are several sample chapters that adequately portray what the rest of the book will be like.

A book proposal is made up of several key elements, including an overview of the book project, an analysis of prospective audiences, a list of comparative book titles and blogs, an explanation of your credentials, a list of marketing ideas, a few sample chapters, a detailed explanation of your writer platform, and more. Think of it as a business document for your book. Better yet, think about it like this: If you wanted to open a new restaurant and needed a bank loan, you would have to make a case to the bank as to why your business will succeed and generate revenue. A book proposal acts in much the same way. You must prove to a publisher that your book idea is a means to generate revenue—you must show that customers will buy your worthwhile and unique product, and that you have the means to reach prospective customers.

As you address why you are the best person to write your book, you'll also lay out the credentials and accomplishments that define you as an expert. Let's take a simple look at where a bio divides between accomplishments and true *platform*. Perhaps you write short fiction stories and frequently submit them to high-profile contests. After several submissions, you receive good news. Huzzah!—you won two impressive short story contests this year. You received a little money, some nice recognition, and a few admirable accolade notes to put in your query/proposal when describing yourself. My question is: How much will these awards help you reach readers when you have a book or e-book available? Very little.

> "As we move into the digital age, platform will be even more important. *How* and *where* authors connect with their readers will affect *how* and *when* readers buy. This has always been true, but there are seemingly more opportunities to influence readers now than ever before."
> —**BERNADETTE BAKER-BAUGHMAN**, *literary agent, Victoria Sanders & Associates*

"Wait," you say. "These credentials matter. If I get a novel published and someone picks it up in a bookstore or sees it on my author website, they could very well read my author bio. And if my bio says that I've won prestigious literary contests it might persuade potential buyers to pull the trigger and buy the book. That's real sales and real money. Isn't that platform?"

No.

Platform is the ability to get people to follow and find you for information and guidance. If someone comes across your website or book in a store by *chance*, that is not platform. Your literary credits will no doubt help you and translate to real money, but they are not platform, in a true sense. Here's what I would do if I were this writer. I would, naturally, use the short story publications as a form of proving my literary cred and hope this translates to book sales. But what I would also do is contact the publications that published my short stories and ask them if they would post news of my forthcoming novel's release online or in their e-newsletter or both.

I'm asking something of the publication, so, as always, I must consider *incentives*. What's the benefit to them in this arrangement? The announcement of my success is a chance for them to brag about how a former contest winner is now a successful published novelist. (Would that make an average random writer take a closer look at entering their contest? It would certainly get my attention.) Said bragging will draw more submissions to their contest/journal, so that means more entry fees (money), subscriptions (money), and submissions (increased quality to choose from). As you can see, it's to their benefit to promote your good news, so they're almost guaranteed to say yes and help you. You, in turn, get your book flaunted to their entire newsletter mailing list or all their website visitors—or hopefully, both.

Bam. You just manufactured platform. Well done.

GOOD NEWS: PLATFORM IS WITHIN YOUR CONTROL

I understand why people don't get enthusiastic about platform building. Writers want to—shocker—*write*, and then (maybe) spend time talking about their writing journey. But building a blog? Tweeting? Volunteering to be a guest contributor to local radio stations? "If I did that, I wouldn't have time to write!" is something I hear writers often say.

But building a platform is the way of the publishing world now. The bad news is there is no secret path to overnight platform success (besides perhaps fame). The good news is that there are some definite bright spots to working on your writer visibility.

Gathering followers and a readership actually gives you a certain degree of control. In the publishing world, many things lie outside your power, such as timing, trends, luck, and the decisions of publishing professionals beyond your sphere of influence. Let me illustrate this point by taking you through different scenarios that follow two possible lives of the same book. Let's say you write a humorous faux memoir written from the perspective of a great white shark. You even have a title for it: *A Shark's Tale: A Memoir*, by Frank Jaws. A publisher has purchased the book (hooray!), and it's set for release six months from now.

SCENARIO 1: An enthusiastic editor buys your book. The bad news is the publishing house lays her off two months later. She leaves the company right in the middle of your editing process. Your shark memoir is then taken over by a different editor, who doesn't get your humor or click with you, causing her to opt out on singing the book's praises during meetings and sales calls. The book is released to little fanfare, sells fewer than four thousand copies in its first six months (a disappointment), and the title is quickly forgotten, forever. Expecting this title to fail, the publisher uses your book as nothing more than a tax write-off. That's it. Your book came and went, and its life is over.

SCENARIO 2: Your enthusiastic editor continues to praise your book in meetings over time—to the point that in-house marketing staffers debate giving it top-tier attention. Two months before your book's release, a completely different publisher releases *The Last Testament, A Memoir*, by God (a real book, published in fall 2011). Guess what? That book sells well and—all of a sudden, by the grace of God (ha)—faux memoirs are *in*. Your book is in the right place at the right time. Now, when people search *The Last Testament* on Amazon, your book comes up in the comparable books below it. Score!

But there's more: Your own publishing house was set to give your book moderate attention upon its release, but is rethinking its promotional strategy with this uptick in presales. Then— hell's bells—another book at the publishing house set for release in the same season is cancelled because of a last-minute lawsuit against it. That book will never see the light of day, so there are resources and personnel who are looking for a new book to publicize. Which one do they pick? Yours, thanks to the book's timely hook and the editor's championing.

But there's more: Three weeks after your book has come out (and is doing quite well in sales, mind you), there are multiple shark attacks off the coast of Florida within a few days. Shark attacks become a hot topic in national news shows, on Twitter, and in Google searches. Thanks to all the focus on sharks, your book sells 75,000 copies in its first six months. It's a definitive success for all involved.

What's the point of evaluating these two very different scenarios? The point is simply to show you that in your publishing journey there will be many things affecting your book—often big things that are out of your control. The four main factors that gave this memoir success in Scenario #2—editor's job security, book lawsuit, God memoir success, and shark attacks making your book topic part of the zeitgeist—are completely out of your realm of influence. You couldn't make them happen even if you wanted to.

While so many things in publishing are out of your control (and this is quite maddening), there is something important you definitely *can* control: your writer platform. Creating a platform is an opportunity to, as social media coach Alexis Grant once put it, "make your own luck." This is, without a doubt, good news. It's why "build your writer platform" is half of my answer to that all-important question I addressed earlier. If you build visibility, buyers will most certainly come. You can't pull the puppet strings on the big events that could shape your book, but you can take control of the day-to-day sales machine that will help you.

The many agents I interviewed for this book loosely agreed that, while it's not always true, a bigger platform will logically lead to a bigger book deal for a writer. That means through your hard work, you can have an impact on the payment a publishing house gives you. The bigger the advance payment, the more the house has invested in a book. The more a house has invested in a book, the more they nurture it and publicize its release to make sure it performs well and makes a return on their investment. The more attention a house gives your book, the more money and book sales you will continue to make. And the more book sales and success you have, the more your platform continues to snowball and the more your future as an author becomes secure.

MORE GOOD NEWS: PLATFORM IS A BREAK FROM WRITING

Many will advise you to sit down and write every day. If you can do this, more power to you. Me? I can't. My ability to write and create (especially fiction) is faucet-like: It's either on or off. Luckily, with the importance of platform building, this isn't a problem. If the inspiration isn't flowing, I can stay busy and further my career by building new contacts. Perhaps you've just completed your latest book and you need a break from writing. Why not hop on Twitter and engage new people? Why not comment on some industry blogs? Keep it fun and simple, and you'll make friends and contacts without trying. Or try some mindless work, such as updating your website. And remember: Platform building is made up of a lot of small steps on a long journey. Every stride helps you get closer to where you want to be.

A word to the wise, though: *Do not get lost in the platform monster.* Platform building can be considered "easier" than writing because it's less complicated than, say, crafting a comprehensive book on the history of gun laws. So it may be tempting to dedicate a disproportionate amount of your time and energy to things like Facebook, LinkedIn, and blogging—but don't forget that platform must be paired with good writing.

EVEN MORE GOOD NEWS: YOU ARE YOUR BOOK'S IDEAL MARKETER

Don't be upset that authors are now their own marketing team. (First of all, this is just the way of the world now and there's not much you can do about it.) While this shift in responsibility requires more time and effort from you, it also points to an interesting fact you should not ignore: You are your book's best marketer because no one on the planet loves or understands it as much as you do. No one can assist your career as much as you can—and that's why being in charge of promoting yourself and your brand isn't such a raw deal after all. Passion and personal relationships will drive your success as an author. That's why making friends and establishing connections—in person or online—is so important.

Consider author Lissa Rankin, M.D., (see the full interview in the author case studies). When her second book came out, she hired a publicist to assist her in getting press coverage. But do you know what dwarfed the publicist's accomplishments? Rankin's own success using her contacts—old and new—to secure coverage about her work. "Even though I hired a publicist, almost every publicity opportunity came directly to me via Twitter and Facebook," Rankin says. "This includes articles in *Glamour, Cosmo*, the *New York Times*, WebMD, AOL, Fox News, *Woman's Day*, CNN, AOL, Forbes, The Huffington Post, and several local TV programs. I've done very little to actively pursue media opportunities, yet, now I get so many."

That's exactly how platform should work. If you make yourself visible and easy to locate in the maze of the Internet, people will *find you*, and you will have to spend less time actively seeking publicity. Again, personal relationships, networking, and likeability trump all.

AND YET MORE GOOD NEWS: OPPORTUNITIES TO BUILD YOUR PLATFORM ARE EVERYWHERE

As you build an online presence and network yourself, get in the habit of thinking: *How can I use this to get me closer to my goals? Is there a way to use this to help my brand, meet new people, or sell books?* Use every opportunity on every level to continue building your house, whether those opportunities are small or big, common or unorthodox.

Consider this: For years, I've posted videos of me playing guitar and piano on YouTube.com (user name csambuchino). Some videos have a few hundred views, many have between 20,000 and 100,000 looks, and one very popular video has somehow collected 2.3 million page clicks thus far. I originally posted the videos online as a labor of love—but as view counts increased, I realized that I could put them to use somehow.

I went into the description for each video and added a small note about my humor book, *How to Survive a Garden Gnome Attack*, then included a link to buy it. I don't know if I've sold five books through my adjustment or 150, but the point is that I am making an attempt to put all my efforts to good use. (And even if 99.9 percent of those who view the note do not buy the book, they do *see the title* and therefore *learn* about the book, building awareness for it. In the world of platform, it all adds up.)

Consider these other varied hypothetical scenarios:

> **SCENARIO 1:** An online article mentions that the local chapter of the Society of Professional Journalists (spj.org) is inviting submissions for its annual journalism awards banquet.
>
> **PLATFORM OPPORTUNITY:** Have you written articles in the past year? Why not submit a few and see if you win an award? (Look for smaller and rarer awards categories to avoid going against a mountain of competition.) If you *do* win an award, you can attend the awards banquet and meet the area's power players in writing and journalism. These are key people to know who can write about your book later ("local coverage") when it comes out. You can also network and try to get more article assignments for the future—spreading your byline to new readers and further building extremely valuable connections. Furthermore, you just technically went from "journalist" to "award-winning journalist"; that's a nice little accolade on top of the platform boost.
>
> **SCENARIO 2:** You run a blog all about local businesses in your hometown of Buffalo, New York, and want to interview three owners of printing companies in a roundup for your site.
>
> **PLATFORM OPPORTUNITY:** If you can convince owners that being interviewed is a great opportunity to spread awareness of their businesses, then you should have no trouble getting lots

of people to speak on the record. So, whom will you interview? Which three business professionals? Here's what I suggest you do: Determine which, if any, business owners are on Twitter. Of those, go after the ones who have more followers than the rest. See, you've already established that the interview is a boon for these individuals, so they will naturally want people to read the piece when it goes online. If they have an online Twitter presence, they will logically spread the word to their followers (or retweet you) to notify others of the post. This way, they get more eyes on an interview about their successful business. Meanwhile, you're getting more page views because you're not the only one promoting the post. Those who were interviewed are actively using their social networks to direct people to your blog, as well. Everyone wins, and you get new followers because of who you strategically chose to interview.

SCENARIO 3: Okay, this last one is not a "scenario" at all, but rather a quick story about when I took over editing a magazine column. After some job duty changes, I was assigned to edit a recurring column in *Writer's Digest* called "Breaking In," which spotlights the debut books of three authors each issue.

PLATFORM OPPORTUNITY: I quickly found out that every debut writer on the planet contacts the current editor in an attempt to get into this column, and that many of the submissions I would evaluate would make excellent choices for the column. A spot in the magazine is highly coveted and competition is fierce. So what was my first order of business? I rewrote the inclusion guidelines to say that all authors chosen for the column would have to write a guest column for my Guide to Literary Agents (GLA) Blog. It wasn't a big change or a drastic request, but it underlines the basic principle of how I am always seeking out opportunities, especially if I have any kind of leverage. If any authors wanted to be featured in the magazine, they would have to guest post for a Writer's Digest blog (mine) when their spotlight ran. They still got what they wanted, but they had to contribute something else small—and those guest columns equal page views and long-tail search results (visibility) for me. Win-win.

I want you, by the end of the first section of this book, to adjust your eyesight. I want you to be able to see platform everywhere—because it is indeed all around you, in myriad opportunities.

AIM TO BE THE RULE, NOT THE EXCEPTION

Now that we've gone over how platform helps you control your own destiny, I feel compelled to mention something: *Platform is subjective and imperfect.* I cannot guarantee that everyone who creates an "impressive" platform will get twenty books published while everyone who exerts minimal effort will never see their work in print. I wish it worked exactly like that, but it doesn't.

The truth is that there will always be exceptions—and you'll read something online at some point from a writer who refused to promote and still got published. Good for him. What I want to impart is that this person is an exception to the rule. And it's not my philosophy to urge people to be exceptions, no more than it is my philosophy to tell you to buy lottery tickets or hit the roulette table if you're short on cash.

If 90 percent of nonfiction writers are getting published in big part due to platform efforts, then guess what? 1) You need a platform, and 2) your hard work will more than likely pay off. Don't cling to some strange exception or aberration and think you won't have to give it your all to find writing success. Trust me—*you will*. "Writers need to be told that this is the journey every writer takes. There is no magic pill," says Patricia V. Davis, author of *The Diva Doctrine* and *Harlot's Sauce*. "The gods will not smile on you and make everything perfect. Those who made it have worked really hard to get where they are."

PLATFORM VS. PUBLICITY

Platform and *publicity* are interconnected, yet very different. Building a platform is what you do *before* a book comes out to make sure that when it hits shelves somebody buys it. Publicity is an active effort to acquire media attention for a book that already exists. In other words, platform typically falls upon the author, whereas (hopefully) a publicist will handle publicity. Publicity is about asking and wanting: *gimme gimme gimme*. Platform is about offering value first, then receiving because of what you've provided and the goodwill it's earned you.

Do something right now: Go to Amazon.com and find a book for sale that promises to teach you how to publicize your books. Look at the comparable titles below it and start scrolling left to right using the arrows. (Do it now. I'll wait.) Tons of them, aren't there? It's because so many authors, especially the many self-published writers out there, are looking for *any* way possible to promote their work. These writers have got a book out—and now they realize copies aren't selling. Apparently selling your work online isn't enough to become a successful writer. That's why you must take the reins of your own platform and marketing.

Once you've found success and lined up a book deal with a traditional publisher, there's the question of what promotion and marketing *you* will actively do (platform), versus what an assigned publicist will tackle (publicity). You don't want to duplicate efforts, step on each other's toes, or misinterpret what your role is throughout the process.

Concerning this advanced perspective, I turned to Hector DeJean, publicist for St. Martin's Press: "There are a lot of things the author can do better than [an assigned in-house] publicist, especially regarding personal contacts, knowledge of the market in which the author is presumably familiar, etc. The publicist typically has a broader understanding of receptive media, ideas about how to promote a book beyond reviews and interviews, and experience about what has worked well in the past for similar books and authors. An author might have some contacts that would be more receptive to hearing from a publicist. So the author and publicist need to get together early on to divide up the work."

Keep in mind that DeJean's aforementioned perspective pertains to the in-house publicist assigned to your book who, naturally, works for you without charge. Finding a freelance publicist is an entirely different task that you should approach with caution. Publicists are not cheap, and you want to make sure you get a return on your investment. It's not good enough to simply have your book e-mailed to a massive list. My best advice is to get a referral from someone you trust.

PLATFORM VS. CREDENTIALS

As I mentioned before, the most important question you will be asked as you try to get your nonfiction book published is: "Why are you the best person to write this book?" This question is two-fold, as it inquires into both your credentials and your platform. To be a successful author, you will need both, not just the former.

Your education and experience weigh heavily when others make a determination of your expertise. For example, if you want to write a book called *How to Lose 10 Pounds in 10 Weeks*, potential readers will wonder if you're a doctor or a dietician. If not, then what gives you authority to speak on your subject? Others will question the advice you're presenting if you do not have convincing expertise.

Would you buy a book on how to train a puppy from someone whose only credential was that he owned a dog? I wouldn't. I want to see accolades, leadership positions, endorsements, educational notes/degrees, and more. I need to make sure I'm learning from an expert before I stop questioning the text and accept it as helpful fact.

All this—all your authority—comes from your *credentials*. That's why they're so necessary. But believe it or not, credentials are often easier to come by than platform.

Platform, as we now know, is your ability to sell books and market yourself to your target audience. There are likely many dieticians out there who can teach people interesting ways to lower their weight. But a publishing company is not interested in the 90 percent of them who lack platform. They want the 10 percent of experts who have the ability to reach readers. In other words, editors want experts who possess websites, mailing lists, media contacts, a healthy number of social media fans/followers, and a plan for how to further grow their visibility.

Book authors are born where credentials *meet* platform.

Please understand this discussion is not to say credentials are irrelevant. On the contrary, they are quite important. Platform will ensure you are visible and have a fair chance to market your book effectively. But credentials will impress readers once they do come to your site—and therefore it's credentials that will seal the deal.

Five years ago, I was giving a speech called "How to Get a Literary Agent" to a small conference crowd when someone raised his hand and asked if I had an agent, considering I was teaching others how to get one. I replied "no," and several people in the room laughed. It completely took the wind out of my speech.

I was taken aback by the laughter. First of all, I was dispensing good instruction, and I was an editor for Writer's Digest Books. What did it matter if I had no literary agent or three different ones? It's still the same speech no matter what. Secondly, I had yet to write a novel or a book proposal—meaning I had *no reason* to have an agent at that point in my career. But none of this logic mattered to the percentage of the crowd I had lost in the blink of an eye. All they heard was gibberish coming from the mouth of some schlep who had yet to walk the walk. They not only wanted instruction, they wanted a teacher who was a battle-tested pro—and anything less was unacceptable, period.

Nowadays, when I give any speech at a conference, I inform people early on I have fourteen published books under my belt and not one but *two* agents working for me (one for books, one for film scripts). My accomplishments give me needed authority, and my authority is what drives people to buy my books and follow my blog.

THE NECESSITY OF PLATFORM

Is it possible for you to sell nonfiction by an author who has no platform? Have you tried any unique approaches to combat this hurdle?

"It's not impossible to sell nonfiction for an author with little or no platform, but the bigger the platform, the better the chances of placing an author with a reputable press."
—**SHAWNA MOREY** *(Folio Literary Management)*

"I think it's extremely difficult to sell a nonfiction book by an author with no platform. Occasionally, I will take on someone who I think has great potential to grow their platform or someone who I think meets a need in the marketplace, but I will not send out a book until I feel comfortable with where their platform is (I'd liken it to serving a dish that is undercooked). The real exception for me is memoir. Sometimes, with memoirs, the writing is so beautiful and the story is so moving that you feel confident it can overcome the hurdle of having no platform."
—**ALYSSA REUBEN** *(Paradigm Literary)*

"It's important for writers to know that the publishing decision is a group decision with publicity, marketing, and sales having active voices and taking a close look at the platform (especially in our post-Borders market). Some recent bestsellers, though (continuing the long tradition), were originally articles in major publications—my favorite being *The Tipping Point* [by Malcolm Gladwell, which appeared] in *The New Yorker*. When a talented writer or researcher has a limited platform, I encourage them to get published via articles in magazines, journals, and content-based websites, and get validation for their work to show that their topic can be of interest to a community of readers/buyers of their potential book."

—**JOHN WILLIG** (*Literary Services, Inc.*)

"It's possible, but it's not as easy as it used to be. When I sold William Alexander's memoir, *The $64 Tomato* (Algonquin), he was just a man with a really big garden and a very funny manuscript. He had no bylines. No expert gardening credentials. It wasn't the easiest sell at the time, and I don't think it would be any easier now. These days, if I like the author's idea but she has no platform, I lay out specifically what she needs to do to build the foundations of one. Sometimes that means submitting pieces to magazines, or designing a logo, or investing in a brand-new website. But truthfully, I pay a lot more attention to platform than I used to."

—**LAURIE ABKEMEIER** (*DeFiore and Company*)

"I've managed to pull that off a few times and it's an uphill battle, but it can be done. When there's no real platform, you usually have to stress the unique concept and the gap it will fill in the market, and the authors have to have very strong credentials. We sold *Welcoming Kitchen: 200 Delicious Allergen & Gluten-Free Vegan Recipes* based on its strong concept and the fact that the meals were actually good tasting and kids would love them. The fact that co-author Megan Hart is the head dietician at Chicago Memorial Children's Hospital gave a lot of credibility to the fact that the meals were thoroughly reviewed for their safety.

"Finally, an approach that an editor taught me herself to sell a book in the case where there is no platform is to show how the topic is trending, and create a convincing list of publications putting out articles, websites, talk shows, and whatever you can find—all very recent, and if you can, building in frequency."

—**GINA PANETTIERI** (*Talcott Notch Literary Services*)

HOW MUCH IS ENOUGH?

You may be asking yourself: "How much is enough? How many Twitter followers is 'impressive'? What would you call a 'solid growth rate' for a website?" and so on. I understand that we all want to set a goal, and thus see a light at the end of the tunnel to strive for.

The first thing you need to realize is that this question of "enough" will be different for everyone depending on the writer's niche. If you're writing about something specific—say, *eclipse chasing*—then your audience is quite a thin slice of the pie, and a smaller platform may be quite impressive in your very specific arena. If you're writing about something broad and popular, such as *finance*, your platform will have to be decently large if you hope to impress an agent.

The size of your desired book deal also factors in. If you dream of getting paid $50,000 or $100,000 upfront for your book, then your platform must be large enough to warrant such a large advance. If your goal is simply to get a book *published*—even if that means with a smaller press that pays little—then platform demands can drop.

All that being said, let me share some very broad thoughts on what you should be aiming for. These numbers below are directed toward writers of *nonfiction*, where platform is crucial and mandatory. If you're writing *fiction* (where platform is not necessary but still helpful), you can strive for statistics lower than the "Notable" thresholds below and still appear attractive to publishers.

BLOG PAGE VIEWS

NOTABLE: 20,000/month
VERY NOTABLE: 100,000/month
IMPRESSIVE BY ANY MEANS: 500,000/month

TWITTER FOLLOWERS

NOTABLE: 5,000
VERY NOTABLE: 15,000
IMPRESSIVE BY ANY MEANS: 50,000

NEWSLETTER SUBSCRIBERS
NOTABLE: 5,000
VERY NOTABLE: 20,000
IMPRESSIVE BY ANY MEANS: 100,000

PUBLIC SPEAKING APPEARANCES
NOTABLE: Speaking to 1,000 people (total) a year
VERY NOTABLE: Speaking to 3,000 people (total) a year
IMPRESSIVE BY ANY MEANS: Speaking to 15,000 people (total) a year

SALES OF PREVIOUS SELF-PUBLISHED BOOKS
NOTABLE: 2,000+ for fiction; 4,000+ for nonfiction
VERY NOTABLE: 6,000+ for fiction, 10,000+ for nonfiction
IMPRESSIVE BY ANY MEANS: 15,000+ for fiction, 30,000+ for nonfiction

WHEN IS A WRITER READY TO SUBMIT?

How large does a writer's platform have to be before they're "ready"? When can they submit with some confidence?

"I think a lot of that is going to both depend on and determine what level of publisher your book is likely to appeal to. There's no 'critical mass' of platform, and in many cases, there's going to be a natural plateauing of what you can achieve at this stage since platform feeds the book feeds the platform. Very large commercial publishers are hoping for, and can attract, writers with large national platforms like nationally syndicated columnists. You may be unable to achieve such an accomplishment before you want to submit your book, or your ideal publisher may not require such lofty extremes for your platform. What *can* you achieve? You may not have a regular column in a big magazine, but if you sell regularly to a number of large publications, mention the readership of each in your proposal. Maybe you're blogging for The Huffington Post. Perhaps your short stories aren't coming out one every three months from big publications, but you've got one a month from some smaller magazines going out to really avid genre readers. Make the most of the assets you have. The way you present what you do and have can be very convincing. Are the pubs you write for very supportive of their writers? Do they tend to do big interviews and reviews of books?

"Some things you should keep in mind ... Don't sacrifice a timely story to continue to build platform and perhaps miss the most opportune window to submit the book. And don't assume a long history is better than recent history. Publishers want to see recent platform, recent exposure."

—GINA PANETTIERI (*Talcott Notch Literary Services*)

"It's helpful to remember that not everyone who is part of your audience will actually buy the book—let's say 10 percent, for example (not a real number, by the way). So if you have 100,000 followers (ten thousand copies sold), it's a lot more appealing than five hundred followers (fifty copies sold). And if you have social media, speaking engagements, and TV appearances, they can only help. For social media, I will start to be impressed when a writer has about five thousand followers/fans/people, but ten thousand is really ideal. Speaking engagements should happen frequently and for a substantial audience. What I look for is national and international appeal, but that can start with regional and local opportunities."

—ROSEANNE WELLS (*Marianne Strong Literary Agency*)

"For nonfiction, I'd say you have to be a recognized expert in your field to get a book deal these days. Your name/your business name/your blog name alone—your brand—should be a shoe-in to sell books. People will pick up the book because of your brand alone. That typically translates to tens of thousands of interactions online or as a speaker. One thousand Twitter followers just isn't really there. Ten thousand? … getting there."

    —**MEREDITH BARNES** (formerly of Lowenstein Associates, Inc.)

"This is a really good question. I've had projects I've been interested in or maybe even have signed up with the understanding that there's work to be done in the way of building or improving the platform before a publisher will be interested. When you can take a project out and have an expectation that it won't get shot down on the basis of platform is a judgment call (as is *which* publishers will feel there's enough platform there, and whether more is necessary to target the ideal publisher). But there's no real answer for 'How much is enough?' The platform is something that should be constantly (if incrementally) growing and evolving over the author's career. Even if one of my authors already has a great platform, I will forward him or her any contact or idea I think may be useful to make it even stronger. I can recall at least one author who accused me of constantly 'moving the goalposts.' She said that she'd done what I'd asked and now I was asking for more. But that's missing the point. There isn't a line in the sand that you need to get across. It's demonstrating your involvement in—or even your necessity to—the world you are writing about. And that isn't any one thing."

    —**STEPHANY EVANS** (FinePrint Literary Management)

"You can never have 'enough.' Part of the business of being an author is constantly growing your platform. A good way to avoid being overwhelmed by it is to write a marketing plan for yourself [as an author] and set achievable goals. A few small actions per day really add up over time."

    —**BERNADETTE BAKER-BAUGHMAN** (Victoria Sanders & Associates)

"Ideally a book is the next step in the author's career trajectory, not the first step. There are fewer authors who are able to build a platform based on a book. Publishers are not interested in acting as a stepping-stone (again, I'm talking about nonfiction). Publishers are better at taking advantage of someone's existing platform. If you're asking a company to pay you to write a book, you have to show that you're bringing more to the party than words on a page. You have to demonstrate that you can bring a piece of the audience with you."

—**LAURIE ABKEMEIER** *(DeFiore and Company)*

CHAPTER 3

THE 12 FUNDAMENTAL PRINCIPLE∫ OF PLATFORM

I can only spend so much time in this book examining each individual platform avenue (blog, Facebook, and the others) available to you. While such explanation may help you *now*, who knows what the key planks of platform—especially online—will be in five or fifteen years. Technology is changing rapidly, but at the core of what we're all trying to do are fundamental principles of promotion, marketing, and networking: twelve principles, in fact.

No matter what platform options you engage, the guiding principles of effective visibility remain the same. The only thing that matters is to find what channels work for you—and to attack them with energy and passion.

Developing a platform requires a multifaceted approach. Consider how several legs hold up a table. What you will learn in this section is that your exact channels and means of platform growth are yours to choose. But what you must do is follow the twelve fundamental principles of platform. If you apply them to everything you do, then the specifics won't matter—and you'll have a good chance of building a better platform, faster.

1. IT IS IN GIVING THAT WE RECEIVE.

In my experience, this concept—*it is in giving that we receive*—is the fundamental rule of platform, and it will reappear in every chapter of this book, over and over again.

Building a platform means that people follow your updates, listen to your words, respect and trust you, and, yes, consider buying whatever it is you're selling. But they will only do that if they like you—and the way you get readers to like you is by *legitimately helping them*. Answer their questions. Give them stuff for free. Share sources of good, helpful information. Make them laugh and smile. Do what they cannot: gather information or share entertainment of value. Access people and places they want to learn more about. Help them achieve their goals. Enrich their lives. After they have seen the value you provide, they will want to stay in contact with you so they can receive more information. They will begin to trust your content—and become a *follower*. And the more followers you have, the bigger your platform becomes.

Always remember: If what you're doing seems difficult, it's probably valuable—and most people will not take the time to tackle difficult, valuable projects. That's what will set you apart and make your content special. If you choose to do so (and I hope you will), that's where you will gain an edge. That's where you will demonstrate value, and takeaway value will translate to platform in the long run.

> "Success ultimately will depend on how valuable potential readers view whatever it is you are blogging about, tweeting, etc., so one of the biggest mistakes is not spending the time and resources to craft an appealing message and content in a

very crowded and noisy marketplace."

—JOHN WILLIG, *founding literary agent of Literary Services, Inc.*

Outside of family and friends, people will not follow your updates or communicate with you for no good reason. You must give them motivation. Like the book *Freakonomics* sought to teach us, what makes the world go round is *incentives*. At every turn, you must consider incentives—i.e., what is the motivation of this person to read my blog/answer my e-mail/help me out, and so forth?

No matter what you're writing and no matter who you are, life becomes a lot clearer when you approach an exchange with other people knowing they're most likely wondering one thing: *What's in it for me?* You will need the help of many people if you want to sell books, people like bloggers, industry pros, other aspiring writers, members of the media, and more. Realize that if you want them to help you, it helps if you can help them in turn—or if you have a lasting friendship with them.

I remember a writers conference where an attendee asked if she could interview me on the topic of blogging. She was starting a new blog and wanted to pick my brain about good blogging practices. Without hesitation, I replied, "No." She looked crushed, so I clarified my answer: "Why don't you post our interview on your blog and include my bio and some book covers? Do that, and I'll be happy to help." Of course, she readily agreed, and I did the interview. As a new writer, it was obvious she was bright-eyed and gung ho, but hadn't stopped to consider the crucial effect of incentives and providing value. If she asks me to take thirty minutes to tutor her for free, I can't say yes. If she says the tutelage will double as an interview that can be posted online to promote the GLA brand and book, then I'm all ears.

While "giving," for the most part, refers to providing content or instruction or entertainment, the concept also translates to *literally* giving items away. Can you give away a portion of your proceeds to a charity? The gesture will generate goodwill toward your project, and the benefitting charity or group will be inclined to help you promote your work. A tipping point for me in blogging was learning about book giveaways. I noticed how guest posts on my site that included a free book giveaway to a random commenter attracted more page views and comments than those that did not. So, while it's not mandatory for guests who blog for me to give a book away, I always tell contributors to "Ask your publicist if they can send out a free copy of the book as a prize." Everyone wins in this scenario. The publicist is happy to donate one free copy in the name of good promotion. The writer's post now becomes more valuable because instead of simply offering content, she is offering content *and* a contest, thereby generating incentive to comment on the post and get involved with my blog. And I get increased page views (and increased platform) because of all of this. Everyone gave, everyone received.

> "If every time you open your mouth you're talking about yourself or your wonderful book, people are going to start avoiding you like the plague. Think of everything you're doing not in terms of how this is going to benefit you, but how it's going to benefit *others*. When you're giving people what they want or need, they're going to want to be your friend. They're going to want to help you."
>
> —GINA HOLMES, *founder of NovelRocket.com, and author of the novels* Crossing Oceans *and* Dry as Rain

Another tipping point for me—this time in the public-speaking arena—was when I recently started to inform event coordinators of my promotional abilities. Years ago, when I would introduce myself over e-mail to a writers conference, I informed them that I could present to their attendees if they would have me at the events. My value was clear: I provided writing/publishing instruction to aspiring writers.

Then, as my blog page views and Twitter followers began to increase, I started, naturally, to use those channels to mention where I would be speaking in the future. After I began meeting attendees who came to the events specifically because of my social media mentions, I realized that I had additional value beyond instruction: promotional ability. Now my pitch to conferences is two-fold: My value (*what I can give*) is 1) an ability to provide expert instruction, as well as 2) spreading the word about their event.

At every step, I aim to increase my value by giving more. And the more I can give, the more attractive I become to invite as a speaker. And the more places I get invited, the more my platform increases and the more books I sell. It all builds upon itself.

Consider your own blogging goals. What are you going to blog about? If you say, "Probably my writing journey and maybe just my general thoughts on life," then you may be in trouble. If you want me as a follower, you have to *give me something*. I need an incentive to take time out of my day to follow your postings. My fellow Writer's Digest editor Brian A. Klems writes a blog called The Life of Dad (TheLife ofDad.com), which is filled with stories about his adventures raising three young girls. Why do people follow his blog? Simple. He entertains them. He makes them laugh. He provides value by giving them happiness, and because he *gives* to them, he will find that many of his column followers (like me) will be inclined to buy his book when it comes out.

Hopefully by this point you're starting to see that what's important is the essential principle: *It is in giving that we receive.* The channels (platform building blocks) and specifics you choose will not matter. Give people an incentive to follow you, and they will.

2. YOU DON'T HAVE TO GO IT ALONE.

Creating a large and effective platform from scratch is, to say the least, a daunting task. But you don't have to swim out in the ocean alone. You can—and are encouraged to—work with others. Don't be afraid to team up with amateur or experienced professionals who are seeking the same goals you are. Many opportunities to latch onto bigger publications and groups that will get your words out can be found. And when your own platform outlets—such as a blog—get large enough, they will be a popular source for others seeking to contribute guest content. You will find yourself constantly teaming with others on your way up, even after you've found some success.

Consider my previous point regarding the value of giveaways. More basic than a discussion of giveaways is a discussion of guest blogging. After I worked on my Guide to Literary Agents Blog for a few years, its size became impressive as it reached the eyes of many writer-readers each day. At that point, it became attractive for other writers (usually novelists) to compose guest content for the blog in exchange for promoting their books and websites in the column. Now, instead of me writing all of my own content (which would take so much time), most of it is written for me. Excellent! And those writers who create content for me get the spotlights and book promotion they seek.

If you're starting a brand new blog, why do you have to be the only one to found it? Why not consider teaming up with others who share the same focus? Perhaps you're trying to sell a book on gardening, so you're brainstorming an accompanying garden blog to increase your platform. Can you get in contact with two other up-and-coming garden writers who want to create and manage the blog with you? That way, the content for the blog is now tripled. Everyone rises together at once.[1]

Let's go back to the dad blog from Brian A. Klems. He, like so many others, simply created a blog on Blogspot.com. But where he rose above other bloggers was in his goal to have other parenting websites carry his content—even for little or no money. Now Cincinnati.com (*The Cincinnati Enquirer*) and other regional newspaper websites print his articles. These are large hubs with built-in audiences. They want good content; Klems wants to be read. Collaboration benefits all. Any money he gets from these outlets carrying his work is merely a bonus. The goal here is not money, the goal is *visibility*. To his credit, Klems achieved his goal and received a book deal for it; Adams Media will release *Oh Boy, You're Having a Girl* in late 2013.

---

[1] If you choose this approach, you're gaining visibility at the expense of personal branding. Some writers will be happy with the tradeoff, others not so much.

There are significant upsides to working with others in building your platform. When reaching out to anyone, just remember Principle #1 and show them what the value is for both parties in the collaboration. You're, in fact, making their life easier—and they will logically green-light your idea and work with you.

Keep all this in mind when planning where you will get the content for your book itself, as well. Whom will you quote? Whom will you interview? Whom will you ask to be involved? Everyone who has a part in the book is, ideally, a marketer for the book due to his or her involvement. After I started gathering images for my 2012 humor book, *Red Dog/Blue Dog*, a great thing happened. People who had contributed photos for the book asked to know when it would be out so they could tell their friends. I realized I had a small 140-person dog-loving army standing by to spread the word! I am anything but going it alone on my journey.

If you're nervous to reach out to others—for anything from a quote you need to an interview you want—know that if you have presented a clear incentive for them to participate in a project or endeavor with you, then most people will help you if they can.

3. PLATFORM IS WHAT YOU ARE ABLE TO DO, NOT WHAT YOU ARE WILLING TO DO.

I freelance-critique nonfiction book proposals for writers, and each of these proposals has a marketing section. Whenever I start to read a marketing section and see bullet points such as "I am happy to go on a book tour" or "I believe MSNBC will be interested in this book because it is controversial," I stop reading—because the proposal has a big problem.

Understand this immediately: Your platform is not pie-in-the-sky thinking. It is not what you *hope* will happen or maybe could possibly hopefully happen sometime if you're lucky and all the stars align when your publicist works really hard. It's also not what you are *willing* to do, such as "be interviewed by the media" or "sign books at trade events." (Everyone is willing to do these things, so by mentioning them, you are making no case for your book because you're demonstrating no special value.)

The true distinction for writer platform is that it must be absolutely what you can make happen *right now*. Consider these:

> **WRONG:** A writer says, "I will start a blog after you buy my book."
> **CORRECT:** A writer not only has a blog, but has a blog that possesses an impressive growth rate and/or has been featured in the media.

> **WRONG:** A writer says, "I think the media would be interested in my book and topic."
> **CORRECT:** A writer explains how the media already is interested in his book and topic, and lists outlets that have interviewed him thus far.

> **WRONG:** A writer says, "I will reach out to celebrities who also campaign against childhood diabetes to get blurbs for my book."
> **CORRECT:** A writer informs you that they've already reached out to celebrities and received callbacks from managers of both Celebrity #1 and Celebrity #2, both of whom have expressed initial interest in helping with the project. Furthermore, the writer already has a confirmation that HelpChildrenWithDiabetes.com will put up a banner ad about the book for a minimum of thirty days when the book is released, because the writer has offered to contribute a portion of the book's proceeds to the American Diabetes Association.

If your nonfiction book proposal demonstrates a lack of realistic, current platform means or efforts, then your marketing suggestions actually work *against* you—because they are not in place right now, and that proves you don't understand how platform works nor what a publishing house looks for in an author.

However, all that said, know that you can—and should—include conservative predictions for your future platform based in reality. Because your book will come out one to two years after you get a book deal, your platform will logically grow during that time, provided your energy is high and said platform has already grown thus far because of its solid foundation. It wouldn't be gauche of you to say any of the following, for example (provided the notes are very much true):

- "I spoke at two industry events in 2011, and already have three on the books for 2012—one of which will have more than two thousand attendees. I am confident that I will speak at no fewer than five events in 2013."
- "My Twitter account now has 15,000 followers, and my overall number of followers is growing at a rate of 7 percent per month. At this rate, my account should exceed 22,500 followers by the end of the year." (In reality, the figure of 22,500 actually only shows the 7 percent growth for six months; a year's growth would be higher—but since you are indeed speaking of possibilities and not realities, you should always aim conservatively.)
- "Since I added my two recurring guest bloggers, my blog's page views have doubled. I intend to continue this successful trend by adding two to four additional guest bloggers over the next year in an effort to increase page views by at least another ten thousand."

But just because you can speak of the future does not mean you should lean heavily on such a crutch. It's only garnish. The main course has to be what you have already worked hard for and put in place. Speak mostly of what you can do—and what you can put into place right now. That's why you need a platform *before* you sell a book.

THE GOOGLE MICROSCOPE

Do you find yourself Googling prospective clients? What are you looking for? How often do you find it?

"If you provide your website, or say that you are on Twitter or Tumblr, I will look! I always research possible clients, not only to see what they've been working on, but also to see if there is a lack of information on the Internet, or potentially controversial or harmful information. An editor will Google the author, and I don't want to be caught unawares as to what they might find."

—**ROSEANNE WELLS** (*Marianne Strong Literary Agency*)

"I do use Google at times to get more information about people who have queried me. I may be looking to verify information in their query or to check on their professional background. I also have a pool of sources who can verify the veracity of someone's book, no matter what it's about."

—**GINA PANETTIERI** (*Talcott Notch Literary Services*)

"Yes, definitely. I'm looking for a presence online (managing what pops up when someone Googles your name is very important!). If I see a Twitter/Facebook/blog/website (not necessarily all of those things), it lets me know that the author is engaged online and what kind of savvy they have. A publisher will really want the author to help (a lot) with promo, so if the author isn't already active in the spaces where that will happen—i.e., social media—then I know it's going to fall to me to teach them to use social media and harangue them into using it."

—**MEREDITH BARNES** (*formerly of Lowenstein Associates, Inc.*)

"I do Google prospective clients. I want to see how present they are on the web, if any dirt comes up immediately, or if there is anything interesting that the author hasn't mentioned in their correspondence with me. I often find some bit of information that helps inform my decision—usually in a good way."

—**BERNADETTE BAKER-BAUGHMAN** (*Victoria Sanders & Associates*)

"I always Google prospective clients. I like to see how active they are online and what news outlets have featured them (the more, the better). I also look for their personal website, a blog, how active they are on Twitter, etc. I even use tools like Tweetreach and Klout to see what kind of impact their social networking has. I would expect any editor who receives his or her proposal to do the same."

—**ALYSSA REUBEN** *(Paradigm Literary)*

"I always Google potential authors before signing them up. I need to know how well received they are by the audience they are hoping to write for. Unfortunately you can't take at face value what people say in proposals. You have to validate information."

—**REGINA BROOKS** *(Serendipity Literary Agency)*

"I always Google. Always. Usually at the query stage. I'm looking for how that person presents him- or herself online. Are sites updated? Are they sloppy or professional? Are they complaining about agents and publishing? (That's a red flag.) I'm also looking at whether I can find the person at all. Sometimes I can't, and that's almost always an instant pass."

—**LAURIE ABKEMEIER** *(DeFiore and Company)*

"Sure—I'm looking for how they present themselves, anything that's raised my curiosity in the query letter, anything that smacks of excitement around them or their subject. I'm not usually looking for something that may have been swept under the rug, but occasionally I do see something that makes me think, *Okay, this is a pass.*"

—**STEPHANY EVANS** *(FinePrint Literary Management)*

4. YOU CAN ONLY LEARN SO MUCH ABOUT WRITER PLATFORM BY INSTRUCTION, WHICH IS WHY YOU SHOULD STUDY WHAT OTHERS DO WELL AND LEARN BY EXAMPLE.

I don't know about you, but, personally, I learn from "watching and doing" better than I learn from reading. A few years back, I was checking out someone's random blog post filled with tips for querying an editor. It was a fine article, but it was dry and too much like so many other pieces I'd read before. I wasn't learning anything. I remember thinking, *What I really need is a big pile of actual query letters that got writers their agents. If I could gather such a collection of successful queries, then by sharing them with other writers, those writers could learn by example, rather than by the usual instruction.* Incidentally, those thoughts were the impetus for a series on my GLA Blog that highlighted actual letters that got writers their reps—and now this "Successful Queries" series is one that I often get complimented on.

So if you learn by example, like me, you'll find some great stuff in the last third of *Create Your Writer Platform*, where I take an in-depth look at twelve different published authors (eight nonfiction, four fiction) who built amazing platforms from scratch. These long interviews examine what worked for these writers, good practices they recommend, and more. Plus, since each writer has a different area of expertise, their paths to success are different—giving readers more approaches to study (and possibly follow/mimic).

On that note, don't be afraid to mimic what others are doing. To see what's working, go to the blogs and websites and Twitter feeds and newspaper columns of those you admire—then take cues from what they're doing. If you notice that your favorite large blogs include all of their social networking links at the tops of their pages ("Find me on Twitter," "Find me on Facebook"), then do the same. If people are getting lots of comments and reader interaction doing book reviews of young adult fantasy novels, why not do the same? Feel free to use Google in this regard. If you're trying to carve out an identity as a guru on saving money, look for the top-branded people in this niche and even a few up-and-coming bloggers who are gaining steam. Study their platforms and see if there are any tips you can pick up.

There is no shame in studying what the best are doing and learning from it. In fact, I recommend it. To better your writing craft, you read the best and slowly learn what works in their prose and why. Think of writer platform as a similar approach. Take public speaking as an example. Giving presentations and sessions is a great way to build a brand, gain authority, and boost your visibility. So if you're speaking on the topic of health, let's say, use Google and YouTube to find other successful health speakers and see how they make their presentations and engage an audience. But don't stop there. We can all be better public speakers by paying attention to the speech patterns and story structures of pastor homilies, standup comedians, and TED.com talks. Keep your radar up and learn from everyone.

5. YOU MUST MAKE YOURSELF EASY TO CONTACT.

If I had to pick one of my biggest frustrations as an editor for Writer's Digest Books, it's the fact that so many writers make themselves difficult to contact. I cannot tell you how many times I've wanted to help someone or promote a book or interview an author only to fail at finding their e-mail address. At least a dozen times, I've found a great debut author online whose book I wanted to include in my recurring *Writer's Digest* column ("Breaking In") but I couldn't. Why? No e-mail. No Twitter. No contact information. Plenty of times no website at all. They don't make themselves available, and I find someone else to interview instead. (Makes you wonder—perhaps you missed out on an easy promo because you kept your e-mail hidden.)

I have no idea why people make themselves difficult to contact. I think it comes from some sort of outdated fear that if their e-mail is online, someone in Chechnya will steal their identity or they'll be deluged with spam. Take it from me—this will not happen. I make myself very available through all channels and am in a position to help people, but the amount of cold-contact e-mails I get each month is small and manageable.

Always remember that your end goal is the creation of a successful writer platform. Besides "visibility," another way to think about platform is *reach*. And if your goal is reach, you do not want to limit people's abilities to find and contact you. While I will pass on putting my cell phone number on the Internet, basically everything else is out there: my work e-mail, my home e-mail, my Twitter, my Facebook, my blog, and more.

If you're questioning your own current reach, the first thing you want to examine is what comes up when your name (or your brand theme) is Googled.[2] When people search for you, what greets them? You want your website/blog and Twitter/Facebook to come up immediately. From there, make sure you're easy to contact. Direct people from Twitter to your blog. On your blog, have a clear "Contact" page where your e-mail is displayed. To avoid spam, take simple steps. An easy thing people do when posting an e-mail address online is write it out like this: literaryagent (at) fwmedia (dot) com. Spam be gone! If you're an established author with a communicative fan base—perhaps you write for children—then include a note by your e-mail saying, "While I do read every e-mail promptly, due to the sheer number of them, I cannot respond personally to all messages. Sorry."

Try to check your e-mail each day. Note how I said "check," not necessarily "respond to." You need to make sure there are no pressing matters. Here's the thing writers must, *must* understand: *Editors have deadlines.* We also procrastinate more often than we should. This means that, plenty of times, we contact people at the last minute and need an expeditious reply. Example: In early 2010, I was on a docked cruise ship an hour away from leaving (when we would lose phone reception). That's when I got an e-mail from a *Boston Herald* reporter who wanted to interview me right at that moment about literary agents. Guess where she found my contact info? Who knows? It was

---

[2] If other established authors exist with your name, perhaps use your middle initial or make some other simple adjustment to make your name/brand unique.

everywhere online, because I make myself easy to contact. However, because I was easy to reach and because I check my e-mail often, this opportunity did not slip away. I was quoted in a major metropolitan newspaper—the article mentioned my book and brand—all because I made myself available and had my bio information listed online. This was an urgent request with a very small time window, so it helped that I check my e-mail often.

On a side note, I should mention that if you have a specific reason for keeping your info offline—such as safety concerns—that is totally understandable. I've run into a few authors with crazy ex-boyfriends who have this issue.

But if you're keeping your info locked up for no reason, please realize that your name and your reach is your platform. You want people to contact you. You *want* other writers to e-mail from out of the blue. I love it when a member of the media finds my info online and writes me. I don't even mind it when a writer sends me an e-mail with a random question. I've made long-term friends that way—friends who have bought my book and sung my praises to others. It's called *networking*—and networking starts by making yourself available and taking the next step to *encourage* people with similar interests or questions to contact you.

6. THE GOAL IS TO WORK INCREDIBLY HARD AT FIRST, THEN LET YOUR PLATFORM RUN ON AUTOPILOT.

If you've ever looked into getting more work done in less time, you may have read *The 4-Hour Work Week* by Timothy Ferriss. One of the main themes of that book is the need to automate yourself, so that work can constantly be done on your behalf with little to no interaction from you. As you will see, the ultimate goal of a writer platform is much the same—to create visibility that helps you sell books and get readers every single day—whether or not you're actively working on your platform. This goal is not as far-fetched as it may sound. In fact, a lot of my own platform is automated at this point, and I will explain how the foundation you build can lead to others performing work *for* you.

It all starts with the fact that the bigger you get and the more content you have archived online, the easier it is to grow, amazingly enough. Besides my own Twitter (@chucksambuchino), I also am one of the lead tweeters for our work account (@WritersDigest), which has 300,000 followers.[3] That's a whole heck of a lot of people listening to us. As we developed the work account, I started to notice something interesting: Even though we tweet fewer daily links as the years go on, our numbers not only continue to grow, but they grow even faster now than they did before.

What this means is that it's easier to build platform when you *have* platform. It's like what Charlie Sheen said about celebrity: "The more money you make, the more things people want to give you for free. It should be the opposite." Writer's Digest gets a hundred new followers a day even when we don't have time on that day to share as many articles of value as we should. *That's* autopilot. The bigger your platform becomes, the more effortlessly it will grow.

Consider what happens when your platform becomes impressive in its niche. You can use that as ammunition to get a book deal—a huge tipping point in your journey. And what happens after you get a book deal? Your platform will grow more—because you have a book coming out, and therefore, more credibility in your specialty. And that increased platform will allow you to sell a second book for more money. With hard work, everything snowballs.

Concerning the idea of autopilot, know that I blog less frequently now than I did two years ago, but my site still gets large numbers of page views (more than 100,000 a month) because I have valuable content that's constantly being found through Google and other search engines. By this point, I have five and a half years of posts on the site— almost two thousand total. That's tons of archived content that turns up in search engines every day, and people from all over the world find me when searching for agents or how to get published.

Not only am I still getting page views because my archived content lets me lean toward autopilot, I'm also selling books somewhat on au-

---

[3] As of the writing of this sentence.

topilot. With every post I put up on the GLA Blog, the post automatically adds a suggestion for a Writer's Digest product to buy—many times the *Guide to Literary Agents*. People come to my large archived site to learn (get value) whether I am blogging or not, and some purchase a book after arriving.

Plus, now that my blog has substantial size, most of my columns are written by guest columnists, thereby decreasing my workload. Young writers have even agreed to interview literary agents for my site for free in the hopes of building relationships with those agents. Again: Once you have a track record of success and size, doors open all around you. It's a wonderful thing to be able to outsource a task or duty and free up your time for bigger initiatives.

When I began speaking at writers conferences, *I* was the one reaching out to organizers and making a case for myself. Now the conferences contact *me*—many times it's a cold contact via my e-mail address. I can only assume they've asked other organizers around the circuit for recommended presenters. That, or they find my blog/website and see my qualifications. Either way, I'm finding public-speaking success because I 1) give the conferences value, and 2) make myself easy to locate and contact—both being fundamental principles of platform. The end result is, instead of saying yes to any event in an effort to build my résumé (like I did five years ago), now the conference must make a case that convinces me it's worth my time to come. Success.

If you're contacting media outlets looking to get interviewed, know that it's easier to secure a media interview *after* you've already been interviewed. The fact that you've already been interviewed proves to them that you're worthwhile enough for a respected media outlet to feature and you can speak eloquently on television. It's the same way with print outlets covering your book. Let's say you're a magazine editor reviewing quirky garden-related books to feature in an upcoming issue. Would you feature my book, *How to Survive a Garden Gnome Attack*? Perhaps. But what if I asked you if you wanted to feature my humor book, *How to Survive a Garden Gnome Attack*, which has already been featured by *Reader's Digest*, *The New York Times Book Review*, *USA Today*, *Variety*, and AOL News? You're probably more inclined. Since the book has already had good coverage, members of the media begin to note that this is something to examine more closely. They figure it must have *some* value since other publications of size wrote about it.

Maybe you decide to collect a bunch of helpful information on a topic—let's say, "How to Market Your Indie Music Record." This will be the hard part; you will have to gather information, verify said information, interview people, read articles, read books, and educate yourself to the max. But when you're finished, you have ideally put together wonderful content that will legitimately help people make money and achieve their goals. In other words, you now possess something of *value*—so make sure you spread this value across all the media channels you can. Just like I will mention later when I talk about article writing, know that one good idea goes a long way. Now that you have the content, you can do the following with it:

- Create a blog post, or many blog posts (a series)
- Tweak the post's slant/angle and use that "new" post as guest content on another site
- Create a small PDF download of the entire article (and perhaps charge a fee for it, or only allow newsletter subscribers to see it)
- Use the content as an event speech
- Repurpose the content as a webinar speech
- Repurpose the content for a class you teach
- Tweet interesting tidbits from the content
- Verbalize your content in front of a camera to create vlogs (video blogs) and video instruction

This is autopilot in action. You worked hard at the beginning and created valuable content that no one else has. Once you possess that value, you can use it over and over again, getting maximum benefit (money/platform) with minimal new writing efforts.

You will see this "work hard now and have it pay off later" theme throughout this book. When you sit down to write your first article query letters or send your first e-mails to prospective guest bloggers, creating such correspondence will take time and concentration. But after the template is built well, you will find yourself mostly cutting and pasting old queries and invites, simply changing a few details to make the notes personal.

To close this point, I want you to understand that while things will get easier as you go along and autopilot options will present themselves, all the visibility you receive must be put to good use. So five hundred new people visited your site today?—congrats. Did they sign up for your RSS feed? Or your Twitter? Or nab one of your e-books on Amazon? Because if they didn't decide to permanently follow you or spend money on your products, they may never return—and you've lost an opportunity.

When people find me through Twitter, Facebook, or a speaking engagement, I lead them to my blog, because that's where most of my tutelage (value) is and also because that's the place where I encourage them to buy my books and attend my webinars and find me at other conferences. My goal is not only to build a writer platform, but also to monetize the platform by selling my products and myself. Others channels you may find me through will lead you to my personal website (chucksambuchino.com), which clearly displays my books as well as my editing services. Keep in mind: Your primary goal is to have people find you, but that's just the beginning. Once you have a platform, you must use it to sell your books (either self-published or traditionally published). Show them value everywhere you can, and then direct them to where they can get even more of the content they like—your books, services, and social networks.

7. START SMALL, START EARLY—AND HOPE FOR TIPPING POINTS.

People who speak disparagingly about writer platform say it's a catch-22—that you can't sell a book without platform, but you can't grow a platform without a book. This is not true. The fact is that while it would be significantly easier to create a platform if you had a book to boost your authority, building a platform from scratch is more than feasible (it's just difficult). If you're having a hard time believing it can be done, just ask the case study authors at the back of this book. The most frustrating thing about building a platform is that you won't have success overnight. Building a platform is like constructing a sky-scraper. In the end, it's a beautiful structure, but it didn't manifest in a day or a month. The journey begins slowly, and your first few steps will be unimpressive.

"The good news here is that no matter who you are, there is a great deal you can do to produce an effective professional image within your book's area of concern," says literary agent Sharlene Martin, in her book, *Publish Your Nonfiction Book*. "Every bit of public exposure that you generate becomes another building block in the structure of your platform."

I won't lie—the first months are rough. They're chockful of effort without a whole lot of return. Fear not; this will pass. Some days you can work your butt off and not see any results, but don't forget that you are closer to your eventual goal. I know the frustration of researching something for eight hours, but at the end of the day not crossing any-thing off your list. Don't forget that you spent the day *learning*—and learning what to do and what not to do is a *huge* part of building your platform. You're on the right track.

If I were you, I wouldn't even wait to finish this book to get your-self on Twitter or start a simple website. Building a platform is an in-cremental process. If you're truly in this game for the long haul—I'm talking years—then you will find great success. If you continue to take steps and build everywhere, you will go nowhere but up.

Like a lot of nonfiction writing, platform is a stepping-stone process—and a lot of this book's case studies reflect just that. An au-thor agrees to speak for free at some local events. She does a great job and gets great reviews. Using those testimonials as ammunition, she is able to book bigger local gigs for a little bit of money. Again, she gets great reviews and praise. She then uses these (better) testimonials as (better) ammunition to land some (better) speaking assignments for (better) money. And so on and so forth.

Let's say you want to build your platform by 1) getting more sign-ups to your e-newsletter, and 2) teaching online webcasts, podcasts, and/or webinars. But you're just starting off and these tasks are frustratingly difficult. What's a writer to do? Address both problems at once by offering people a free on-demand (prerecorded) webinar if they sign up for your newsletter. With a new, impressive incentive to sign up, your newsletter list will expand more quickly. Secondly, if your webinar is dynamite, then it's only a matter of time before someone who has a connection to a teaching program somewhere (like at Writer's Digest, for example) downloads it and passes your name along as a new instructor to hire. In this case, you will have moved toward achieving both your goals at the same time.

Resist the urge for instant gratification. Small steps are not bad. You must always consider what an action has to offer and whether it can lead to bigger and better things. "What frustrates most people is that they want to have platform *now*," says literary agent Roseanne Wells of Marianne Strong Literary. "It takes time and a lot of effort, and it builds on itself. You can always have more platform, but trying to sell a book before you have it will not help you."

My job is not to teach you how to avoid small steps, but how to avoid *missteps*. In other words, how to avoid small steps that do not clearly lead you to bigger, more productive ones. Your goal is to work efficiently and to forever be pushing in the right direction. Along the way—and you never know how or when these will come—you will hope to arrive at tipping points, as well as great successes that raise your platform to the next level.

These tipping points and successes are few and far between, but they're exactly what you're after—a payoff that can generate platform/revenue for you. My former boss Jane Friedman tweets news about e-media and the publishing industry. Someone at *Publishers Weekly* magazine was enjoying her tweets, because they suggested Friedman as one of five people in publishing to follow on Twitter. What do you think happened to her number of followers after that? If you made a sound equivalent to a slide whistle going up, you are correct.

Her Twitter followers number started to increase—fast. That was a tipping point for her. And after she had gathered tens of thousands of followers, people who came across her profile randomly couldn't help but be impressed that she was so popular, so they followed her, too, knowing that she must be providing some great value to get that much attention. And with that, we're connecting Fundamental Principle #7 (start small and grow) with Fundamental Principle #6 (the goal of autopilot).

I don't want to spend too much time "teaching" you how to bring about tipping points, because they are, to a large degree, outside your control. You don't know when a celebrity is going to retweet you—but you *can* do simple things to make your tweets easily searchable (and therefore more visible) on Twitter. You don't know when a blog post is going to go viral—but you *can* dedicate yourself to creating great, unique content that will rise to the top.

So if you find yourself writing a column for free or speaking to a room with only twelve people in it, don't fret. These are just the first steps.

8. HAVE A PLAN, BUT FEEL FREE TO MAKE TWEAKS.

At first, uncertainty will overwhelm you. What are you going to blog about? How should you present yourself when networking? Should your Twitter handle be your full name or the title of your book/brand? All these important questions deserve careful thought early on. The earlier you have a plan, the better off you will be in the long run—so don't just jump in blind.

The more you can diagram and strategize at the beginning, the clearer your road will be. Just because your first steps will be simple and small doesn't mean you shouldn't immediately attempt to find your footing and establish your niche—i.e., what you want to focus on and become an expert in. Building a platform means creating a brand around your name and book. A big concern as you build your platform will involve establishing your niche(s) of expertise as well as your desired end goals. These are *huge* things to figure out. Before you can become a noted expert in something, you must define what that "something" is. Before you set off into the wild world of social media and platform building, I want you to decide what your final goals are. Pinpoint your goals and brainstorm the necessary step-by-step paths to achieve them.

Don't skip these steps when building your platform early on. *Map out a plan. Set goals.*

What was my own goal? To be able to write nonfiction books. At the beginning, I didn't even realize I wanted to write humor books. I originally set out to build a platform around all my writing titles. My strategy mostly involved blogging frequently, doing a lot of public speaking each year at writers conferences, and writing articles for a host of local publications. When social media came around, I signed up and slowly began seeing the value of it—so I implemented the use of sites like Twitter and Facebook into seeking the end goal of publishing titles on writing and publishing. My strategy now utilizes more elements, but all roads led to what I wanted down the road: to gain authority and sell books.

It all sounds easy when I write my journey out like that. But the truth is, my plan endured *countless* tweaks along the way, as I continued to discover more about 1) what I wanted, 2) the best route to get there, and 3) changes in how information is shared as time went on. I expect your journey to change course based on these same three factors.

As you step out and begin creating a writer platform, make sure to analyze how you're doing, then slowly transition so you're playing to your strengths and eliminating your weakest elements. For example, maybe your blog is growing faster than any other aspect of your platform plan. Great! So focus more time on it, if that's where you're seeing the best results. But why stop there? If you have the blogging chops and connections, start guest posting for other large sites. Blogging's what you do well—so play to that strength and ditch something that's not working. Multiply your strengths to multiply your successes.

No matter what you want to write about, no matter what platform elements you hone in on, don't ignore the importance of *analysis* and *evolution* in your journey. Install Google Alerts (google.com/alerts) so you can find out what people are talking about on the Internet when they discuss your site and your books. Take a look at what you're doing right and wrong to make sure you're not throwing good money after bad. And feel free to make all kinds of necessary changes along the way to better your route. When I say "changes," this could mean anything, big or small. Examples:

- Revise your speeches after you talk so they're even better next time.
- If your weekly blog post, which shows a personal side of you, is getting little to no comments, try a different approach.
- Perhaps you started two Twitter accounts—one as a personal handle and one as the main character from your novel. If your personal handle is growing much faster than your main character, consider whether it's best to pull the plug on the main character's account.
- Continue to beautify and update your website and blog as time goes on.

9. THE WORLD IS CHANGING, AND THE GOAL OF PLATFORM IS TO LOOK FORWARD, NOT BACK.

When we talk of platform in this book, we are looking *ahead*—because, in fact, your book lies *ahead*. (If you're self-published, imagine that your other books lie ahead.) For example, one of the simplest ways to build a platform is to write articles—preferably for websites or magazines within your field of expertise. A handful of people reading this book will stop to say, "Well, I have *that* covered. I wrote more than one hundred articles for large newspapers and publications from 1999–2009."

Ah, but there's one problem: That's all in the past. You need articles coming out in the future—so those who read your articles can then find your book. What's done is done—and editors are only interested in what you *are doing right now* and therefore with what you will continue to do when your book is released and promoted. What has happened in the past is not without value; that all adds up to credentials and expertise (and hopefully connections). But what it does *not* equal is platform moving forward.

Sometimes when I'm teaching, a conference attendee will raise their hand and try to point out a flaw in my platform instruction. It usually goes something like this:

"Wait a minute, Chuck—what do you mean you need a platform and have to take the lead on your own marketing? I happen to know for a fact that the author of *Who Moved My Cheese?* had absolutely no platform—none!—and he's a super-mega bestseller now. So, obviously, your logic is flawed. Case closed. The jury rules in favor of *me*."

"Platform, just like narrative voice and character development, can be subjective, and what I think is going to be enough to sell books might not be the case from editor to editor. It's also important to judge platform against what is currently being bought, what is now on the market, and what the potential for platform is in the future (in other words, what is the advantage, if any, to waiting?)."
—ROSEANNE WELLS, *literary agent, Marianne Strong Literary*

Here are three quick things you should know if you're going to be any kind of professional writer:

1. **NEVER COMPARE YOUR WORK TO A BEST-SELLING AUTHOR BECAUSE NON-BEST-SELLING AUTHORS DO NOT ABIDE BY THE SAME RULES.** Once you become a best-selling author, you can pretty much do whatever you want. If you ever approach an editor or agent and try to justify something you're doing

by referencing how Dan Brown does none of his own marketing, you will immediately lose their attention.

2. **NEVER COMPARE YOUR WORK TO BOOKS FIRST PUBLISHED OUTSIDE THE UNITED STATES, UNLESS OF COURSE YOU LIVE OUTSIDE THE UNITED STATES.** You're trying to embark on a business deal with an American publisher, so don't try to compare yourself to writers overseas. Don't explain to an editor that two of your friends in Barcelona who got business books published had an army of publicists at their disposal, because that's how they roll over in Spain.

3. **NEVER ASSUME WHAT HAS HAPPENED IN THE PAST IS STILL RELEVANT TODAY.** This is the big one for authors who are trying to develop a platform. Here's the gist: ten years ago, an author didn't truly need a platform, but now she does. That's it. There is no way to argue around this fact. I understand it would be nice to go back to the 1980s, when things were easier and Guns N' Roses were still together, but we can't—so we must just move on and work hard.

When mapping your writing journey, look to peers who are active *today*, selling books *today*, using the technologies of *today*. They will be the ones you want to emulate and study. They will be the ones who will make great contacts. They will be the ones who have blazed a path that you can follow.

10. TRY YOUR BEST TO BE OPEN, LIKEABLE, AND RELATABLE.

In this book, you're going to read about a lot of fancy stuff like "retweets," "search engine optimization," "book proposals," and the like. That's all good and well—and all that stuff will help you build your visibility without a doubt—but never forget that in writing/publishing, just like in all walks of life, *it matters who you know.* Seriously. Writing is a business, and just as with any other business, having friends in the right places will open up all kinds of opportunities.

Networking still works wonders—just as it did fifty years ago, well before there was the Internet or social media. The very basic tenet of networking is to meet people when you can, connect and befriend them, and generally just *enjoy* being around other people. In other words, it behooves you to be a warm person. Even if you get nervous speaking in public or lack high-profile contacts in the media, being a warm, authentic person will go a long way in networking and making friends. If your efforts come off as needy, fake, or self-centered, you will not move forward.

> "Building a platform takes time and a lot of hard work. It's like building relationships, because really it *is* building relationships. That takes time and trust. Just because you have three readers today, doesn't mean you fold in the towel and call it a bust—it means you're three closer than you were yesterday."
> —**GINA HOLMES**, *founder of NovelRocket.com, and author of the novels* Crossing Ocean *and* Dry Season

And just as it matters who you know, who you are as a person will also help you gain followers. It's not only okay for some of your personal side to leak out through social media, it's healthy. Otherwise you may seem robotic or cold—more of an information-spewing service than a real human being. Case in point: Despite the fact that I run one of the biggest blogs in publishing, whenever I head to a writers conference, the most common first compliment I get is either regarding my dog, or regarding my posts about my old cover band.

See, I spent about four years playing guitar in a cover band around Cincinnati and shared a bunch of my most amusing stories online. The stories gave my blog an entirely new dimension, as they showed a personal side of me and also added an entertaining, humorous element to the site. And my success discussing my band is by no means an outlier. Co-workers here at Writer's Digest have found success and gained new followers by talking about their children, their taste in shoes, and their favorite brands of bourbon. Who knows? You could get as many page views one month by talking about your love-hate relationship with reality TV as you could with more typical information-filled posts.

So when you're reaching out to others by any means—in person, through Twitter, or perhaps when querying for an assignment—keep in mind that the other person is not only looking at the content of your niche, but also *you the messenger*, whether they consciously realize it or not. While I recommend that you show a bit of your personal side via your platform channels, keep in mind that you should always err on the side of professionalism when engaging pros like agents and editors through social media.

Likeability matters. If a recurring feature on your blog congratulates peers for whom you're genuinely excited, it is bound to boost your likeability. If someone mentions you online and you take time to reach out and thank that person, you'll be perceived as a nice person.

On the contrary, if almost everything on a new writer's blog is focused on *them-them-them* and *buy-buy-buy*, then it actually becomes more difficult for the blogger, because the reader/buyer has no connection to them. The writer appears to be little more than a fame seeker who asks for money and favors at every turn.

Concerning this somewhat ambiguous idea of what it means to be "open" or "warm," I want to share two quick stories that may help you understand how opportunities will hopefully befall those who connect in earnest. In 2010, I went to see Aerosmith in concert. I was in my seat with a friend awaiting Aerosmith's excellence (they can still rock the house, in case you're wondering), when I noticed that the woman sitting next to me looked like a literary type. (Stereotyping? Probably. But bear with me.) I asked her if she was a writer, and she said yes, though I got the feeling that I was annoying her with simple conversation. I asked her what she wrote and she told me, adding that she had yet to see her work in print. Then she asked me a question: "Have *you* ever had anything published?"

Now this is not the easiest question for me to answer because I write books, articles, stage plays, screenplays, and more. So my first word of response was "Uh…" as I prepared an answer. As soon as the woman heard the word "uh," she immediately cut me off and said, "That's a *no*," before turning away and smirking, as if satisfied that I was no better than she was. Even though this was years ago and took up just forty-five seconds of my life, I will never forget it. I could have helped this writer. I could have answered practically anything she wanted to know about how to get her work published. But this was not someone who enjoyed connecting with others—at least from what I could see. She viewed my striking up a conversation as a nuisance, not an opportunity.

If you are trying to build a platform, this is exactly the type of writer you do not want to be. You never know where your next great opportunity or next writer friend for life will appear. Stereotyping, again, this is the type of writer who will blog and tweet out of duty, not choice, and spend too much time complaining about that one agent who didn't return her e-mail or that author who gave "bad" advice. A negative attitude will do you no good—just as using the ease of social media as an avenue to complain and vent will do you no good.

The second quick story happened to me recently and will hopefully demonstrate the other side of the coin. I was on Facebook and saw a random status update that said, "Let's help this woman get to 100 comments." I didn't recognize the gentleman who posted the update and I didn't know what he was talking about—but I'm naturally curious, so I clicked through to a blog column.

The column itself was from an aspiring author who explained that her child's poor health had bankrupted her family, and she was approaching desperation. It was very sad. So many of the comments were incredibly kind; people who knew the writer and even those who didn't offered to send checks and money. I decided to help a little, too, and offered several critiques for writers who would donate proceeds to her. She was grateful for this, and the critiques went fine.

As I did my final critique for charity, I noticed the writer lived in Greece. I wrote back to her and mentioned how beautiful the Greek isles were and how I would love to instruct there one day. Well, wouldn't you know it? The writer replied with a link to a writing retreat to be held on a Greek isle. A retreat she had planned and which happened to be looking for a faculty instructor that summer. After some talk, she invited me to teach on the Greek isle of Ithaca[4] and to possibly come back every year, if things went well. What an amazing opportunity.

This boon did not befall me because I agreed to donate time and money. Many, many people gave more than I did. The opportunity befell me for other important reasons:

1. **I NEVER TURN DOWN A FRIEND REQUEST ON FACEBOOK.** I seek to build my platform and meet other writers. This means being *open*—perhaps even more than most. So I welcome new Facebook friends and converse with them when possible.

2. **I CLICKED THROUGH TO THE COLUMN ALTHOUGH I DID NOT KNOW WHAT TO EXPECT.** This is simply because I'm eager to read new blogs and make new friends. A conversation is not a nuisance to me; it's an opportunity. It's the only way to make connections—and making connections is the foundation of platform.

3. **I STARTED A CONVERSATION WITH THE WRITER OF THE CRITIQUE I DID.** My reply was something like, "Hey, here are my thoughts on your query letter—see below … By the way, I've heard about some retreats put on in the Greek isles from time to time. Those sound great." It was kind of a strange thing to do—transition from business to pleasure like that. But you know what? Every relationship we build begins with some kind of cold contact.

Who you are, how you act, and your basic mind-set on life will play into your ability to influence people and build a platform. If you want success with books, I urge you to strive for openness and reach, and those elements will not come about unless you seek to

---

[4] Retreat website: hwrw.blogspot.com

make connections wherever possible. And that won't happen if all you do is talk about yourself.

You'd be surprised at the success you achieve when you leave your agenda out of communication with others and simply *interact* with those who reach out to you, especially on an individual level. One of my favorite blogs on the Internet is the huge film news site SlashFilm.com. After reading the site for years, it was quite wonderful to see my own name in a post (!) when Sony optioned my humor book, *How to Survive a Garden Gnome Attack*, for film. I wrote the blog's founding editor just to say thanks. He probably had no time to reply, but he did indeed write back to me and was very nice. That made an impression on me, which is probably why I praise his website several times in this book. He was warm and open, and I like to promote/praise those I know who are kind people.

11. BE PART OF YOUR OWN COMMUNITY AND UNDERSTAND THE NEEDS OF ITS MEMBERS.

You can only best understand and help members of your niche/community if you're heavily involved with them. Your goal is to join and participate in any kind of community that links you with those who share your interests—and by *participate* I'm talking meaningful interaction, not status updates on Facebook that tell people to buy your book.

Beyond simply gaining knowledge, the more involved you are with groups and communities of like-minded people, the more people you know who will be aware of your book when it's published. That's platform. And during your entire journey, you won't just be speculating about what information your niche audience appreciates, but you'll be sure you're providing quality content because you *are* your audience.

Make an effort to join one or a few trade organizations related to your niche. Even if there are costs, it's worth it if you get involved and make networked connections. Communities are vertical now—"tribes" of like-minded people, says marketing expert Seth Godin. This means that if you want to find people who love politics as much as you do, you're much better off not searching for a group of people who simply love to read the newspaper (where politics is only one element of a "horizontal" outlet), but rather groups that read politicalwire.com and frequently comment on CNN.com's political blog. These people are concentrated on their niche of choice.

If you don't find an appropriate community, start one. If you're a young adult fiction writer and no chapter of the SCBWI (Society of Children's Book Writers and Illustrators) exists in your area, take the steps to create one. You'll make friends with people who have similar interests, and you can work together to help one another reach your end goals (Fundamental Principle #2). On this note, know that writing groups are a good fit for all writers, not just novelists. Get involved in literary events in your area—book launches, author panels, writing groups, online writer organizations, and more. Volunteer with writers locally to build contacts. "Go to conferences," urges Hector DeJean, a publicist with St. Martin's Press who promotes novelists. "There are a lot of conventions and conferences whose primary purpose seems to be to put up-and-coming authors together with established pros. Authors of all levels trade tips and make friendships, and the veterans often agree to blurb books."

Something (possibly drastic, possibly not) to consider is working in the field you want to be in. Consider even taking a pay cut to go into your specialty industry. If you make the switch, then you will be, in some way or another, building your platform every week by default—by making connections, getting involved, and sharing knowledge.

Remember that the key to an effective writer platform is to build bridges and avenues *before* you need to start using them. If you have a book out now and join some kind of group, do everything in your power not to come off like you joined the group solely to hock your wares. What you want to do, ideally, is give before you receive (Fundamental Principle #1). People who join Twitter and then tweet randomly, saying "Hi, please follow me and check out my book on Amazon" will find little or no success through social media. Signing up for things is easy. Becoming a valuable member of a community is much more difficult and much more important. Don't forget: People innately respect those who have paid their dues.

Also, keep in mind you can always reach out to organizations and communities that you're not involved with—as long as you give them a good reason to correspond with you. (Remember: Incentives trump all.) When I was writing my humor book, *Red Dog/Blue Dog*, my wife suggested that since our own dog was a rescue we should donate a portion of the book's proceeds to a no-kill shelter. It was a great idea and I immediately said yes.

First, this decision generated extraordinary goodwill among other dog owners I contacted. Upon hearing that money from the project would save dogs' lives, people were willing to donate images for free and even spread the word throughout their channels. They owned rescued dogs, I owned a rescued dog; they wanted to help other dogs, I wanted to help other dogs. I was relatable (Fundamental Principle #10), and a member of their tribe.

Second, this donation idea opened an opportunity to partner with a charity organization of my choosing. In theory, the proceeds can be donated to any dog welfare organization. Whichever organization that is will naturally want to mention the book to their members through a newsletter or website. The more the book is talked about, the more everyone wins. Once again, we're back to Fundamental Principle #1. It is in giving (charitable donations) that I'm receiving (promotion assistance).

So study your target audience and determine which specific subcategories of people will buy your book. Then get involved in those groups. In addition, study what your readers like. What do they read? What websites are they addicted to? What TV shows do they watch? Analyze why and aim to provide content created just for that tribe.

12. NUMBERS MATTER—SO QUANTIFY YOUR PLATFORM.

Numbers matter in this business, so you must find ways to *quantify* your platform. If you don't include specific numbers, editors and agents will be forced to assume the element of platform is unimpressive, which is why you left out the crucial detail of its size/reach. Details are sexy; don't be a tease. Consider the differing approaches below:

> **WRONG:** "I am on Twitter and just *love* it."
> **CORRECT:** "I have more than ten thousand followers on Twitter."

> **WRONG:** "I do public speaking on this subject."
> **CORRECT:** "I present to at least ten events a year—sometimes as a keynote. The largest events have up to 1,200 attendees. A full list of events is on my website."

> **WRONG:** "I run a blog that has won awards from other friendly bloggers."
> **CORRECT:** "My blog averages 75,000 page views each month and is growing at a rate of 8 percent/month during the past year."

> **WRONG:** "I have friends in the media."
> **CORRECT:** "Previously I have been interviewed by WVRC-12 in Boston, WKRT radio in Bridgeport, and three AM radio stations in New York City. I have open invitations from all outlets to pitch future interview topics and will do so with this book."

Paying attention to your own numbers is imperative because agents and editors will demand specifics. Also, analyzing those numbers will help you see what's working and not working in your platform plan and allow you to make healthy changes and let the strategy evolve (Fundamental Principle #8). Numbers reflect the success you're having, and it's up to you to figure out why you're having that success.

For example, I noticed early on with my GLA Blog that I was getting a lot of page views on posts about agents for Christian works. I did a little investigating and saw that my site actually came up second on Google when "Christian agents" was searched. I played to this strength and interviewed Christian agents any time I could to soak up more platform and sell more books. If someone else seeking a specific niche would have been blogging and seen this interesting void, they could have carved out a great specialty by being the go-to expert on finding and signing with agents who seek inspirational and Christian titles.

Evaluating my own numbers really helped me in this situation. Specific numbers = what's working = analysis and evolution = betterment of platform.

Detail your platform at every turn when dealing with agents and editors. Saying you're "on Facebook" and "run a newsletter" and "have a newspaper column" is not good enough. If you said that to me, I wouldn't miss a beat in responding, "Yes, but how many Facebook friends do you have? How many people subscribe to your newsletter? Are you already selling books through your newsletter, and how many have you sold with that tool? Is your column in print or online, or both? If in print, how big is the circulation? How often do you write original columns? What are the columns' online page views?"

Most of your information is easy to quantify (e.g., Facebook fans) while some other things require a little research. You may have to familiarize yourself with Google Analytics (google.com/analytics) to get true blog hit numbers, or call up some event/group organizers to know exactly how many people receive such-and-such newsletter—but those little pieces of investigative info are vitally important when submitting your book for the possibility of publication.

I realize there may be a temptation to take platform shortcuts where possible to increase sheer numbers, but beware of what I call "hollow growth." If I come across a publishing pro on Twitter who has ten thousand followers but only follows 350, that's impressive. But if I come across someone who has ten thousand followers and follows fifteen thousand, that's *not* impressive. It points to a situation where the followers aren't ideal "followers," per se (i.e., ones that will spend money on you and your product), but rather people who are following you simply because you're following them. "Weak" followers like these, in my experience, are much less likely to buy your books and listen to what you have to say.

This same basic philosophy and warning translates to Facebook, as well. If you're randomly befriending dozens of people each week, you will slowly but surely get people to say yes and up your friend numbers—but if those new "friends" aren't interacting with you and commenting on your status, agents and editors will make the discovery when they evaluate your platform up close.

Websites like grader.com and Klout.com give your Twitter and Facebook accounts an evaluative grade based on things like how many people are interacting with your content. If you've only established hollow growth and your posts are not being shared or garnering comments/traffic, then your platform numbers will be viewed as somewhat misleading. Even if agents and editors don't worry about your hollow growth, you should. Perhaps you *do* get a book deal and a large first print run results based on your platform numbers. But since the platform specifics were a bit deceiving, your title underperforms. Sadly, those unimpressive sales numbers will stick with you for life. How can you make a case for a second book when the first one lost money?

A bit overwhelming, isn't it? Yes, publishing pros will put your platform under a microscope. They must—to ensure that a solid platform does indeed exist, not a weak framework of one. So provide numbers early and always. And if you're avoiding numbers, details, and specifics because you think your visibility is thus far unimpressive, hey, don't sweat it! Remember that everyone's platform starts at zero. But if you're reading this book, and you're willing to give your platform the time and attention it needs, all will be well in the end.

HEAVEN'S IN THE DETAILS

If a writer skips numbers and uses generalities only, such as they "love to speak on the subject" or "run a nice blog," do you assume, since the statements lack specifics, that the platform is small in these areas?

"I always investigate. I am shocked at how often I uncover important *positive* pieces of information ('I went to Harvard! I know Malcolm Gladwell!') that the author was too sheepish to mention in a query or proposal."

—**LAURIE ABKEMEIER** (DeFiore and Company)

"I think it's a bit of both. Let's say this kind of language is enough to raise suspicions, but I will still have a look, check their site to see if they have a calendar, Google them, etc. Sometimes an author who is querying or who has even submitted a proposal just hasn't got the memo yet that these things really are important. They may have more up their sleeve than they are showing and only need to be asked. Sometimes I make it easy to cut to the chase by asking directly, too."

—**STEPHANY EVANS** (FinePrint Literary Management)

"I assume small platform unless someone links me places or gives me specifics about speaking engagements. If you're proud of accomplishments, you share specifics."

—**MEREDITH BARNES** (formerly of Lowenstein Associates, Inc.)

"It's all about the details, specifics, and numbers. For example, authors and publishers love great endorsers, but now the question is 'Will these endorsers endorse your book directly to their communities (via an e-mail blast, blogging, or reviews), and what is the size of that community?' Again, the buyers/distributors want to know this as much as the publishers. So saying 'I will,' 'I could,' etc., does not count. I represented an upcoming entrepreneurial/sales success book coming out that has more than one million e-mail contacts through the author's endorsers who have promised to promote the work to their communities. Now that gets attention! It's not enough to 'love to speak.' Show me how many times you have spoken to groups the past two years and your upcoming plans/commitments and the actual size of the audiences."

—**JOHN WILLIG** *(Literary Services, Inc.)*

"I'll ask more questions, but it's a mistake to assume that will be the case, so the writer needs to get the details in there on the first pass."

—**GINA PANETTIERI** *(Talcott Notch Literary Services)*

"I will always ask for numbers, as it is concrete proof that I can bring to editors that the book has potential. Having solid numbers also tells me that you have done your research and you are invested in continuing to build your platform."

—**ROSEANNE WELLS** *(Marianne Strong Literary Agency)*

"I would advise writers to be as specific as they can if the information is readily available. Personally, if the subject matter piques my interest, I'll investigate on my own. If the book's subject is already a well-covered topic (diet, relationships, etc.), the author's platform and reach is that much more important. An impressive platform outlined in detail might mean the difference [between] an agent quickly passing on your material to taking a closer look at what you have to say."

—**ALYSSA REUBEN** *(Paradigm Literary)*

"I typically investigate. Many authors don't understand the need for specificity and they also don't understand how vital it is to brag. I have had many a conversation with writers who have appeared to have weak platforms until I had a chance to thoroughly interview them. A treasure trove of platform jewels appears. They often don't understand the importance of things that might seem tangential but really do add significantly to the big picture."

—**REGINA BROOKS** *(Serendipity Literary Agency)*

CHAPTER 4

CHOOSING
YOUR NICHE

Building a writer platform essentially means *being known for something*. So a natural question I'll ask now is, "What do you want to be known for?" In other words, what do you want people to think of when they think of you? Some quick hypothetical examples of influential people you could be or something you could be part of:

- The guy who knows everything about chocolate chip cookies and samples them all over the world
- The girl who blogs all about indie heavy metal music/news
- The instructional site (with multiple teachers) that's all about how to get better at blackjack so you can win more money at the casino

Any one of these is a *niche*. It's a specialty, an area of expertise. People don't achieve recognition and popularity by being okay at something. No average basketball player ever made the NBA, let alone became famous. Your goal is to find a niche and *own* it—with excellent understanding of your content and market, and by providing great material that people can't get elsewhere.

Think about the websites you frequent the most. Why do you visit them on a regular basis? It's probably because you 1) know what type of content they will provide, and 2) you know the quality of said content will be worthwhile. That's called establishing authority in a niche. One cannot be an expert in all things, so instead we pick something specific and learn everything about that specialty. After you choose a niche, you try to become associated with that forte—and from there, you seek to build a *brand*. "Your brand defines who you are to the outside world," says Robert Brewer, editor of *Writer's Market*. "Brand identity is what helps you get to the point that clients are seeking you out, instead of the other way around."

In this chapter, I want to show you the value of narrowing your topic, the importance of branding yourself, and how a niche can help both nonfiction and fiction writers. And remember: No matter what you want to develop expertise and authority in, it will help a whole heck of a lot if you enjoy what you're doing. You will be absolutely shocked to see how much productivity you have when work doesn't feel like work. If you love documentaries and start a website all about news in the documentary world, you will *enjoy* blogging and tweeting and interviewing people and going to events. And when that's the case, you'll get more done than you thought possible.

"Building your brand is just the act of making sure that everything you do to increase your blog traffic works together and helps build you, the blogger/author/person, as a brand with whom people can identify. Being consistent is the surest way to build [platform] over time. Don't try to change your blogging persona every week. Pick an identity and stick with it. That's one of the surest ways to connect with your audience."

—**ROBERT BREWER**, *poet and editor of* Writer's Market

HOW SPECIFIC IS SPECIFIC ENOUGH?

The broader your niche, the more difficult your road ahead. Think about it. What sounds more feasible to you out of these two options? 1) taking six months to establish a website all about how to build your own house, or 2) taking six months to establish a website all about installing a garage door opener. The obvious answer is number two. It's smaller, more focused, more concise, and therefore easier to master and cover all bases.

Let's examine something focused—at least much more focused than, say, a newspaper—the Writer's Digest family. You may say, "Writer's Digest is a focused entity because it's all about *writing*. That's specific enough."

On the contrary, writing and publishing, as a niche, is extraordinarily broad. Writer's Digest produces a magazine, runs contests, has trade books, manages e-commerce stores, plans huge events, edits the market books, and much more. What does it take to keep Writer's Digest running? Dozens of employees working every day. You don't have dozens of employees, so you should not aim to create a website around whole topics such as "writing" or "politics" or "health." These are way, way too broad.

So how do you trim these topics down? Try these ideas on for size:

- Instead of "writing," try the niche "writing about cats or for cat publications/websites."
- Instead of "politics," try the niche "political news affecting Long Island."
- Instead of "health," try the niche "how to build brain power and have a better memory."
- Instead of "seafood cuisine," try the niche "seeking the world's best oysters."
- Instead of "travel," try the niche "the best family-friendly places to visit in the Northwest."

- Instead of "self-help," try the niche "how to recover from emotional abuse."

All six of these sliced niches are now simple, feasible, and clear—and you could easily make them even more specific if you liked. If you carve out something unusual and focused, you will immediately face less competition as you start to develop a platform, and your identity will be easier to explain. If you want to write a broad book titled *Inspire Your Workforce* or *A History of Music*, you're immediately going up against platform behemoths—and publishers know that.

Remember: Your niche can always expand if you want it to. My Guide to Literary Agents Blog's main focus is, you guessed it, helping writers find a literary agent. But a few years into blogging, I started to notice some limitations concerning my niche. First of all, I wanted to post a greater amount of content online; and secondly, people who found success in writing and/or obtained an agent would not return to my blog because it would no longer be of service to them. My solution was to expand the blog's focus and add the topics of "platform" and "promotion." This gave me more subjects to tackle and write about, and also allowed me to provide content to advanced writers who already had an agent. Making this decision increased my site's page views and my book sales. My platform ticked up.

RESEARCH YOUR NICHE

When you carve out your specialty, a large part of your early journey will be researching what already exists. What books tackle your subject? Which ones have sold well? What e-books? What are their Amazon Kindle rankings? Once you've examined similar books, take a long look at blogs in the industry. They are your direct competition.

While you should think outside the bookstore, visits to physical stores are also a wise research move. Look at the shelf of your category (business, architecture, or whatever it may be) and see what's new and what's available. Don't just linger in Barnes & Noble. Brainstorm other specialty stores that you envision carrying your book, such as Spencer's, Guitar Center, or PetSmart. Also, if you're still brainstorming the exact angle of your niche, you might consider whether there is any way to tap into the zeitgeist or a trend you believe to be forthcoming.

> "I'd rather have one thousand readers who are fanatical about children's books than ten thousand hobby readers. Why? Because the conversion rate for the first group is *always* going to be better. And those are the relationships I want to cultivate. Great and *specific* content attracts more dedicated readers who then become better customers."
>
> —**MARY KOLE**, *literary agent and author of* Writing Irresistible Kidlit: The Ultimate Guide to Crafting Fiction for Young Adult and Middle Grade Readers

WHAT IS A "BRAND"?

Constructing a brand is fancy business-speak that translates to being known for something specific. There are two very important parts to that last sentence. You cannot have a successful brand unless you are *associated with something* and you are known. The opposite of a brand would be anonymity in the writing marketplace and Internet. Brands aren't just for Fortune 500 companies; every writer will sell more books if they become associates for providing a certain type of content—such as "gothic horror novels," "simple-to-understand guides on building a website," or "the latest Hollywood celebrity dating rumors." Stay focused on a clear topic for a certain audience. Your book will not be for everyone or even close to everyone—and that is A-OK.

A simple tip as you strive to build an identity is to keep a note above your desk that has your overarching goal written on it. No matter what you're doing, no matter what element of platform or writing you're working on, make sure it ties into that goal on the paper. For example, my core goal is to "help writers get published." Whenever I'm writing something, I always return to my note and question if I'm being true to my brand and giving readers the instruction they need.

While your strategy and niche will evolve over time, it's still best to develop a plan and stick to it (Fundamental Principle #8). If you start a blog and begin tweeting with no clear goal as to what these platform channels will achieve, then those channels will achieve just that: no clear goal. In your quest toward a successful platform, you don't want to be merely "helpful." You want to be an influencer who has some say about your niche topic. Empty blog posts will not get you any closer to authority.

CHAPTER 5

PLATFORM FOR FICTION AND MEMOIR

We've already established that platform is mandatory for nonfiction—but what if you're writing novels for adults or children? And what about memoir? Do you still need a platform for these categories? The quick answer is that while you don't absolutely need one by any means, building a platform will without a doubt help your writing career. It will help you sell more books and control your destiny (as much as that is possible). It also allows you channels where you can reach out to fans and prospective readers. All of these are beneficial to have and will make you more valuable as an author.

Take it from Elana Johnson, author of the young adult novels *Possession* and *Surrender*. Johnson created a popular blog in the writing community and usually gets forty to one hundred comments on each post. (Consistently getting any number of comments on posts—even seven to ten—is a good thing.)

In a blog column where she discusses the upsides of platform, Johnson stated what she thought were the benefits of the hard work she put in before she even had a book deal: "I believe that MTV asked me to blog for them because of my blogging experience here … [and] I believe that blogging has brought me more than $25,000 more on my debut deal. I've done what I set a goal to do: make meaningful connections." And Johnson is not alone in her personal story. Novelists Billy Coffey and Gina Holmes, both of whom share platform advice in this book's author case studies (in the last major section of this book), attribute a portion of their payments directly to the blog platform they created *before* they had a book deal.

Plenty of times, novelists shy away from platform building, saying something along the lines of, "I believe my job is to write a great book and hope that it finds an audience." And just to be clear, yes, this answer is very valid. The number one thing you can do to sell more novels is write a damn good story; the quality of the prose is paramount, according to Beth Gissinger, digital marketing director for F+W Media: "When I sit in title acquisition meetings, it's my job to help ensure we are signing projects from authors with decent platforms. That said, I'd take a chance on a memoir with great writing and no platform vs. a memoir with lousy writing and decent platform most days."

But you must understand that building a platform can only help your success and worth as an author. Think of it from the perspective of a publishing executive. Sales are a bit down, so she's acquiring fewer books and being careful about what gets published. Then an employee appears in her office holding two manuscripts to consider, but notes they can only say yes to one. The executive reads both books, and neither disappoints. Good plots, good characters, good series potential—both of them. The executive can't decide which one to choose. Then she asks the employee about both writers' platforms. It turns out Writer #1 is an enthusiastic guest blogger for some big sites and has 7,500 followers on Twitter, among other accomplishments. Writer #2 actually "hates social media sites" and is "not a fan of being interviewed."

If you were this executive, whom would you choose? I personally would choose Writer #1, and there is no logical reason why anyone else wouldn't do the same thing. The first things an editor looks for in a novel are exactly what you think: quality, salability, and across-media potential. But a certain small factor in their decision-making methods is indeed platform—because your personal reach is *money* for them.

Like nonfiction writers, you can choose old-school methods, new-school methods, or a mix of both. Naturally things like a robust blog and Twitter account will serve you well and get you out there. But note that fiction writers have found a good deal of success with more traditional methods, like making contacts with book reviewers and such. Perhaps that's why when I asked Hector DeJean, a publicist who promotes mostly fiction, to provide his definition of platform, he said this: "This is not a perfect definition, but I would say *platform* is the promotional program that an author supplies before the book is even acquired—connections, scheduled events and affiliations, tie-ins to upcoming media events, etc."

WHAT CONSTITUTES A FICTION NICHE?

Nonfiction writers have a relatively clear route to platform. If a man in Michigan wants to make a name for himself as an expert on restaurants in the state, he can start a blog and Twitter account and newspaper column all about his specialty. Boom. Done. The train is off and running; let's all wish him good luck.

But what's a novelist's specialty? What's a memoirist's niche? These are much more difficult to pin down because often no clear answer exists. However, that's not necessarily a bad thing. Not being forced into one "clear" niche allows a writer to decide what she wants to blog about. It gives writers openness and opportunity. In my opinion, writers of fiction and memoir have three different platform routes they can take:

1. The "loose subject connection" niche
2. The "altogether different" niche
3. The "writing focus" niche

DON'T FORGET THE CASE STUDIES

The entire last third of this book is made up of case study interviews with authors. I asked around for names of writers

CREATE YOUR WRITER PLATFORM

who built effective platforms from scratch. When I got a list of names, I sat down with these authors—a decent number of whom write novels and memoir—and asked them what they did right on their way to creating visibility and a brand. When you're finished with the instructional sections of this book, don't pass up a chance to review what they said.

1. The "Loose Subject Connection" Niche

This approach means choosing a major theme in your book and making that your focus. Perhaps your books always feature detectives of Native-American descent—most of the time solving cases on reservations. You likely have a great interest in Native-American culture, so how can that translate into a blog? Perhaps you can write about news involving First Peoples communities or inspiring stories of what's going on in the West today. Or perhaps you can do some research and share interesting stories from the past that many people aren't familiar with. You're creating content that has a major relation to what you're writing, so those who come to your site and also read fiction would be target readers for you.

Perhaps you wrote a memoir about raising your autistic son. Can your blog be a news site about autism treatment developments? Perhaps it can be a site that collects inspiring caretaker stories? Simply examine your main theme and elements of your book, and brainstorm a website you'd like to see in existence that doesn't exist already.

Here's a loose connection niche in practice: Delilah Marvelle is a successful romance writer who's had many books published. On her blog each month, she posts a true story about sex in the context of history. Her fiction genre is romance, so discussing true stories about sex in history is a fascinating and successful way to build a readership and platform. Not only has it gained her blog readers and friends, but it was this "sex and history" column that caught the attention of a big-time literary agent who later offered to represent her.

2. The "Altogether Different" Niche

This approach is when you simply try to build a platform of some size while acknowledging that it has little or no connection to your novels and memoir. For example, maybe you're a literary fiction writer who is sitting around brainstorming what to blog about. You ask yourself, "What do I love to discuss in life?" Perhaps the answer you keep coming back to is, of all things, *mountain biking*. Okay. If this is your true passion in life and you won't easily get bored writing about it, then I say go for it. Create content with passion and gusto, and build a community around yourself. The goal is simply to create a huge readership and to hope that some of that visibility translates to book sales. No doubt it will, though exact numbers will be difficult to come by.

In a manner of speaking, I myself fall into the "altogether different" niche because I write two distinctly different types of nonfiction books: how-to titles on writing, and quirky humor books. When I started writing humor books, I debated on building a second platform by submitting articles to humor sites and such but ultimately decided against it. My opinion was that my publishing platform was already amply successful in one arena, and the sheer size of it was enough to ensure that a small percentage of people who visited my blog would also buy my humor books. I expected some crossover and am confident there has been plenty.

Having a platform outside your niche runs directly contrary to popular teaching, but it can work. In my case, my humor books fall into a more general category that can be marketed to any group. The goal is that in meeting people online and in person, readers will connect with me through my writing advice, but also get to know *me*, Chuck Sambuchino, the person, the husband, the dog lover, the wannabe rock star, the chocolate chip cookie addict. When that happens, the brand they follow becomes *me*, not GLA. That's the goal. And achieving that goal to some degree or another allows me to sell humor books.

3. The "Writing Focus" Niche

The primary focus of this blog is your own writing journey, along with your personal successes and challenges along the way. These blogs are extremely common with new writers, which means there is good news and bad news if you try this approach.

The good news is that there are plenty of up-and-coming writers who will immediately identify with your subject matter—that is to say, readership exists for your website. The bad news is that there are so many "new writer" blogs out there already. Here's what happens: An unpublished writer writes a book and then hears that he should be online, so he starts a simple blog. He doesn't know what to write about, so he defaults to chronicling his attempts to get published.

What a blogger will likely not realize is that there must be more than five thousand of these "new writer" blogs out there. And that means you are immediately facing stiff competition everywhere in every direction. Remember that you want to carve out a unique niche, not compete against as many people as possible.

These warnings are not to say that this plan can't work. It actually works plenty of times. Look at young adult writer Elana Johnson again. She blogs about writing, does it well, gets tons of reader interaction, and credits a huge chunk of change to her hard work. There are and will continue to be success stories with writing blogs—but beware of focusing only on your writing journey. Brainstorm what else you can bring to the table. I'll start you off with some ideas:

- Can you interview professionals or authors? Stick to a specific niche (e.g., science fiction writers), so your blog/site gains an identity.
- Can you review books?
- Can you round up industry news in a certain genre or subject area?
- Can you answer reader questions? Again, try to be specific. I've seen writers have some success answering questions about "writing about psychology" or "writing about hospitals." These approaches are *specific*—and specific is good.

Try to come up with different dimensions and elements you can give your brand other than "writer trying to make it who wants to update you about their writing journey." It's not very original or entertaining on its own, and so many people are doing it already. Plus, having this focus often makes the blog more for you than for others. It also lends itself to writing posts about the slog of trying to get published, and that might easily include complaints about editors and agents in the industry. [1] Not a good thing to publicly vent!

TALKING PLATFORM FOR FICTION AND MEMOIR

Have you found fiction editors discussing platform with you yet? Taken one step further, have you met any editors acquiring fiction who do not only value platform, but also actually *require* it for a book to be considered?

"Platform has been far less important with fiction, as far as the editors making inquiries about books, but that doesn't mean that the authors haven't been proactive about taking initiative to distinguish themselves coming in, and that's likely going to make a difference going forward. I've yet to find an editor who *requires* a platform for fiction, but many will Google the author if they're interested in him or her. It helps give them something to talk up going into the acquisitions board if the author has a following already or has a really interesting life story that might be buzz worthy."

—GINA PANETTIERI (*Talcott Notch Literary Services*)

"For fiction, platform is more [about] just showing me that you know how to be relevant and use online media, which will make

[1] Remember that you will get Googled. While Dale Carnegie has long since said complaining will often hinder your ability to develop personal relationships, his advice is doubly true now, as your words are searchable and can live forever on the Internet. Agents and editors do not want to be in business with someone who is badmouthing the industry and those who work in it.

you an asset in promoting your book. So there just has to be an active presence, not necessarily numbers."

—**MEREDITH BARNES** *(formerly of Lowenstein Associates, Inc.)*

"You still definitely get more of a pass with fiction—it's really about the story and the author's ability to tell it. But editors are very happy nonetheless if you can show up with a blurb or several from established novelists, or with the promise of a contact or well-placed friend who will see that the book is introduced to a large, relevant group. And there are also a number of editors who have told me they are looking for stories that can be pitched with a news hook, and of course want to know any special connection the author's real life has with the world of his or her creation. In genre fiction, I have had editors ask, 'Are they a member of Romance Writers of America?' or 'Do they attend Malice Domestic?' I'd say, so far, rather than *demanding* platform, fiction editors are extra pleased if the author can contribute platform."

—**STEPHANY EVANS** *(FinePrint Literary Management)*

"For fiction, I've seen a good author platform transform a respectable deal into an impressive deal. Having a name, experience, awards, a built-in audience, and publishing credentials all make a difference."

—**BERNADETTE BAKER-BAUGHMAN** *(Victoria Sanders & Associates)*

"Yes, fiction editors do want a platform—they generally just don't call it a 'platform.' They will say *position*. 'How will we *position* the book?' This is just another way of asking how we plan to get this author an audience. I haven't seen fiction editors actually say that they require a platform, but they will often reject a book if they don't know how to position it. If the author has a platform, this question is silenced."

—**REGINA BROOKS** *(Serendipity Literary Agency)*

Concerning memoir, are editors requiring that writers have a platform? Or does platform merely help their case?

"I'll say this—it could never *hurt* your chances to develop relationships with publications going out to your target audience, and to be an active member of groups that could support your book. There are so many memoirs battling for attention. Some rare few will sweep an editor away just on the voice and story, but always there's a need to determine 'How will we sell this?' 'Who is the readership and how will we reach them?' How can you, as author, help them to see that potential? If your memoir is about cycling across America, and you are a very active and recognized member of large cycling organizations and write for their publications and blog about cycling, you're going to be seen as able to reach your market that much more easily."

—GINA PANETTIERI *(Talcott Notch Literary Services)*

"Memoirs can be sold with no platform, but they have to be extraordinary and extremely well-written, standing out in the market in some way—and even then it's still a gamble. Other published work is important; *Eat, Pray, Love* was not Elizabeth Gilbert's first book."

—ROSEANNE WELLS *(Marianne Strong Literary Agency)*

"With prescriptive books, I think platforms are non-negotiable—but memoirs are a bit of a different case. Obviously, a nice platform makes a book more salable, but if a memoir is beautifully written and tells a completely unique or exciting story, I think publishers are more open to taking a chance on the book and buying it. More and more, it's the author's responsibility to do whatever they can publicity- and marketing-wise to break their book out once it's published, though. So in that year or two between when the book is sold and when it is published, I would suggest the author concentrate on building up their platform. Remember, if a first book fails, it's very hard to sell a second book."

—ALYSSA REUBEN *(Paradigm Literary)*

"It depends on the category. If it's a tough memoir category like parenting/family or coming-of-age, editors are looking closely at not only the writing but the author's connections and how likely the book is to get review attention. Memoirs that fall into stronger categories that are also inherently gift-y (e.g., food, pets, and gardening) have an easier time overcoming the platform issue."

—**LAURIE ABKEMEIER** (*DeFiore and Company*)

"In my book *You Should Really Write a Book: How to Write, Sell and Market Your Memoir*, my premise is the following: The most commercially viable memoir authors have a hook, a platform, and exceptional writing. If you come to the table with two out of the three, an agent or editor will help you get the third."

—**REGINA BROOKS** (*Serendipity Literary Agency*)

BECOME A MEDIA EXPERT

Being quoted in the media—especially in large outlets—does fantastic things for your platform. First of all, you can mention these credits in your bio ("She has been quoted by the *New York Times* and CNN.com). Second, every time that you are quoted in the media, there will likely be a tag behind your name explaining who you are and what gives you authority to speak ("...And that's how you get an agent," says Chuck Sambuchino, editor of *Guide to Literary Agents*). The more media outlets you're quoted in, the more you increase your influence, authority, credibility, and visibility.

To get your comments in the media, it helps to network and befriend people in the media. Besides that, the first obvious tip for achieving your goal is to develop a good website with key search terms so that your name comes up when reporters Google phrases ("expert on seismology," "world's best video game players"). A second piece of advice is to sign up for and participate in websites that seek out expert sources for news stories. Sites like this include:

- Help a Reporter Out (HARO) (helpareporter.com)
- ProfNet (profnet.prnewswire.com)
- ExpertClick (expertclick.com)

Sites such as HARO have "paid" and "unpaid" subscription options, with the former, naturally, being more valuable. If you pay for such a site, make sure you're getting your money's worth. If not, cancel your subscription.

Beyond sites that seek sources and experts, keep an eye out for two other kinds of media opportunities: 1) local media outlets, and 2) blog talk radio. Can you contact a regional radio program and offer to be a free contributor in your specialty? Perhaps you're writing a book about music. Can you get airtime every Friday talking about what interesting musical groups are playing each weekend? Also, many small blog podcasts look for quality guests. Google some keywords—"blog talk radio" and (your niche)—and reach out to program hosts with a proposal to be a future guest. There may be few listeners catching your words, but being a guest on the radio ups your credentials, and you can later embed the finished audio on your website as a sample of your speaking skills. If someone with influence hears the recorded website audio and reaches out, you may have just stumbled upon a tipping point (Fundamental Principle #7).

6 TIPS ON BUILDING A BRAND

Sidebar provided by Robert Brewer (robertleebrewer.blogspot. com), editor of Writer's Market *and* Poet's Market.

Carving out a niche as an editor who understands the publishing industry has afforded me several opportunities that other editors have not received. Likewise, branding myself as a poet with a popular blog has led to my being named Poet Laureate of the Blogosphere. I was also invited to be a National Feature Poet at the 2011 Austin International Poetry Festival. Building a brand is easy on paper, but it requires rolling up your sleeves in real life. Here are six simple tips:

1. Make a list of who you are as a person. Are you nice? Are you helpful? Are you outrageous? Are you funny? Are you authoritative? Try not to answer yes to every question you ask yourself.
2. Make a list of who you are as a writer. Answer the same questions above. Hopefully the answers align with step 1.
3. Define how you'd like others to view you. Again, it would be nice if this aligned with steps 1 and 2.
4. List your writing specialties and successes up to this point. It's okay if you don't have a long list.
5. List what you'd like to do with your writing in the short term. Then begin working toward these goals while keeping in mind how these goals align with steps 1 through 3 and/or build off step 4.
6. List what you'd like to do with your writing in the long term. In a perfect world, this will build off step 5.

The main thing you want to do is identify who you are and who you want to be. Then everything you do should be an extension of this identity. I would strongly advise against dramatically changing who you are in an attempt to find success. Instead, build upon who you are by emphasizing your strengths and working on your weaknesses.

THE MECHANICS OF PLATFORM

CHAPTER 6

PLATFORM AVENUES: WHICH SHOULD YOU CHOOSE?

Earlier in this book, you can see my list of what I believe to be the ten biggest platform planks. Which routes you will take are completely up to you—and everyone's paths will be different, as everyone's goals and target audiences are varied. I would say two things are mandatory: 1) you must create a website, and 2) you must get started in some channels of your choosing, though you control which ones. As you start to develop the different prongs of your platform, here are a few key comments to keep in mind.

YOU SHOULD NOT DIVE IN EVERYWHERE. That's right. I am officially telling you not to tackle every opportunity or go down every path. It's much like firing in all directions without really aiming—and it is a surefire way to accomplish less and run yourself ragged. With platform building, "more" can be good, but it's often not. In fact, "more" can dilute your channels' effectiveness and cause complications rather than payoffs. Pick a few avenues and develop them to the fullest. Your goal is to delve deep in one or several ways, rather than skim the surface of everything. "It can become very easy to be sucked into *everything* that has to be done and therefore none of it is accomplished correctly," says Beth Gissinger, former head of publicity for Adams Media. "If you have limited time/resources, focus on only a few elements of your online platform and execute them consistently. If you're picking where to spend your time, I would say a great website is vital (with a blog and SEO attention)."

YOU CAN CERTAINLY MIX OLD-SCHOOL AND NEW-SCHOOL METHODS. I am a big believer that you should stay on top of the times and utilize new methods (Google+, Facebook), but also stick to tried-and-true approaches (public speaking, participating in groups). Mixing avenues is a healthy approach. Just because the world is technologically advancing and there's a new social network every year doesn't mean that "old-fashioned" methods are obsolete.

> "Advertising can be an enormous expense for authors that, in the end, doesn't generate any sales. There's a reason why publishers don't typically do big ads for debut authors, even the ones they really believe in. The best thing for an author to do is to figure out which specific things have worked for previous similar books, and which are just expensive sound and noise."
> —HECTOR DEJEAN, *publicist for St. Martin's Press*

NO ONE WILL AGREE ON THE BEST WAY(S) TO PROMOTE. Building your platform is about finding what works for you while limiting your time wastes. Even the literary agents who weighed in throughout this book sometimes disagreed with each other. This is perfectly normal, and it all depends on what you're writing and what works best for you.

YOUR AUDIENCE WILL NOT RESPOND WELL TO RELUCTANCE, AGGRESSIVE SALESMANSHIP, OR A GENERAL INABILITY TO PERFORM A TASK. If you signed up for Twitter and have no real interest or belief in it, then it will show through your tweets, without a doubt. The same goes for anything else. "If you're iffy on blogging, I say don't do it," says Mary Kole, literary agent at Movable Type Management. "There are too many bad blogs, blogs about people's cats, blogs about the day's word count, blogs by people who think they need a blog out there already. Don't add one more to the pile. Blogs by a clearly reluctant author are the worst."

When I personally meet another author on the Internet or in person, here are three things I never want to think during our exchange:

1. This person seems to be reaching out to me not out of want, but out of *duty*. I can tell they don't want to promote themselves, but they're doing it anyway.

2. The only thing this person cares about is selling to me, and it's starting to get annoying how many times I'm being told to check out his book.

3. This person seems nice, but she doesn't speak well in public. She needs to find a new way to connect with people.

"You want to put the emphasis on what you do best—writing, teaching, speaking, self-promoting, social media—and what you enjoy the most. But also be willing to be out of your comfort zone and learn the skills necessary to create the platform."
—**ETHAN GILSDORF**, *national freelancer and author of the memoir* Fantasy Freaks and Gaming Geeks

KNOW THAT YOU WILL BE GOOGLED BY PUBLICISTS AND AGENTS AND EDITORS. So the question is: What do you want to come up when people search for you online? Obviously, the platform elements you dive into will be your top search results. Unfortunately, so will other things you do not want popping up. "I Google authors all the time," says Beth Gissinger, digital marketing manager for F+W Media. "I'm looking to make sure the author hasn't been bashed in the press for something—something that could come back to haunt me when I'm pitching the book."

Wondering about this subject this very moment, I just Googled myself. The top results that came up that I could immediately see (the six results before you have to scroll down) are the following:

- My personal website
- My Guide to Literary Agents Blog
- A Writer's Digest Shop landing page all about the *Guide to Literary Agents*
- My Twitter account
- My profile page on Amazon, listing all my books
- My Facebook page

These are good search results. If you're not happy with what comes up when your name is Googled, get yourself out there with websites and social network profiles and interviews. Build them up, and they will become your natural top results.

HEY, WHAT ABOUT THAT OTHER THING?

Due to space limitations, I can only address the biggest platform avenues in this book—specifically a website, a blog, a newsletter, article writing, public speaking, Twitter, and Facebook. I consider these to be the most important, and therefore worth the special attention and instruction.

What you will quickly notice is that plenty of newer social media channels such as Etsy or Pinterest or Ning are not discussed here (or at least not at length), but you should by no means ignore them or think them of no value. Evaluate every opportunity and study whether it has potential for a good return on your time investment. Pay special attention to anything that's built specifically for your specialty or niche, such as a social media site for health professionals, business professionals, or professional magicians—if that's up your alley.

WHAT'S THE MOST IMPORTANT PLATFORM AVENUE?

Do you have an opinion on what type of platform development is the most important (blog, Twitter, newsletter/e-mail list)? Or is it not that simple?

"It's not that simple. It depends entirely on the type of project that writer has created and where that reader tends to be found. For example, cookbook buyers love blogs. So creating a great blog and doing blog tours where you can be a guest on some popular blogs (and trying to get a nice cross-section of different types of blogs for different audiences) would be very helpful. You have to study your readership and determine where they 'live.' I do suggest writers try working with everything and see where they're getting the strongest response and then focus on that. Create a Facebook fan page, tweet several times daily, build an e-mail list, and diligently take a stab at blogging."

—**GINA PANETTIERI** *(Talcott Notch Literary Services)*

"Platform is never simple, and every type of platform helps. Speaking engagements, social media presence, membership in your industry's groups and affiliations, previous publications, and national television and radio appearances all lend themselves in strengthening your platform."

—**ROSEANNE WELLS** *(Marianne Strong Literary Agency)*

"The most important platform is the one that allows you to engage with the media and your readers in the most authentic and organic way possible. For some people, social media is the best way to do that. Some of my clients, especially the artists, have great success connecting with fans and building their platforms at fan shows (such as comic cons or craft fairs, depending on the book) or through selling wares on Etsy. I've seen clients build huge early audiences by putting together interesting projects on Kickstarter. For fiction: Publishing with journals or magazines, or getting involved with online writers' groups or forums, are great options. My advice is for authors to seek to engage with readers and media through the avenues that are most accessible and enjoyable for them."

   —**BERNADETTE BAKER-BAUGHMAN** (*Victoria Sanders & Associates*)

"I think it totally depends on the type of book you're selling. If you're pitching a book based on a blog, the blog traffic should be high enough to garner a book sale. Traffic indicates to publishers that there is a ready-made audience out there for the book. When you show that traffic is substantial and is continuing to increase, that's even better. Whereas for a more prescriptive book, I think Twitter, speaking engagements, and newsletters may be more important than just website traffic. When presenting an author's platform, the goal is to give the complete picture of an author's reach and potential."

   —**ALYSSA REUBEN** (*Paradigm Literary*)

"It's all integrated. The Barnes & Noble buyer and others will be interested in how many potential customers can be reached through e-mail newsletters/book launch campaigns, Facebook and LinkedIn friends, and Twitter followers that will help drive interest in the book/topic and to their stores/websites. That's the *digital* side. How many speeches and workshops an author presents and the size of the audiences is all taken into account and is of equal interest, depending on the publisher. Articles in leading publications and/or shorter web articles/blogging are valued as they can go 'viral' within these buying communities and have the potential of going global. The author's ability to

appear on TV or radio (or even better, host their own show) is a 'platform' capability, too, and highly prized."
    —**JOHN WILLIG** *(Literary Services, Inc.)*

"The best type of platform is the one where the author feels the most comfortable. Publishers are thrilled to see an author who can do Twitter, a blog, an e-newsletter, Facebook, and a podcast if the author can do them all well—but few people can. I've had directors of publicity or marketing say that they'd rather have an author do one thing perfectly than three things half-assed. It's less important what you do than how well you do it."
    —**LAURIE ABKEMEIER** *(DeFiore and Company)*

"I don't feel that there is one platform that is most important. The key to effectively utilizing one specific [platform] or multiple platforms is [to] know and understand your target audience."
    —**SHAWNA MOREY** *(Folio Literary Management)*

CHAPTER 7

YOUR WEBƧITE: THE FOUNDATION

Let me start this chapter by simply saying that if you don't have a website, *get one now*. While I suggest waiting a little while to blog or tweet because you need to refine your niche and set goals, you can start immediately on a website. Everyone needs one. It is the foundation of your platform, and even a minimalist-yet-professional website provides two things immediately: 1) basic, important information about yourself and what you write, and 2) a means to contact you (Fundamental Principle #5). Your most vital tool in possessing reach through the Internet is a website.

Your website should be, as editor Robert Brewer puts it, "your central hub." From there, you use commands (note the active verbs that follow) to direct people to do things such as *enter* your contest, *buy* your books, *sign up* for your newsletter, *listen* to your last webcast, *visit* your blog, *follow you* on Twitter, *connect* on Facebook. Make sure that when people come to your web page that they don't slip away forever. Encourage them at every turn to connect with you in some way for the long haul.

Know that, in this chapter, by "website," I do not mean merely a blog. A blog (discussed in depth on in Chapter 8) is one fluid page that is constantly filled with new content. A website is a landing site that has different, crucial elements on various pages—such as information about yourself, your work, and your books/services.[1] A blog may be one prong of your website, if you want to keep things nice and simple.

No matter how you approach constructing a website, know that while you may very well be able to put together a site yourself, make sure it gives off a vibe of professionalism. "Uncomplicated" is a fine term to describe your site, but you don't want it to look cluttered, clunky, or ugly. Invest in your website and yourself, so that those who reach out to you will immediately see who you are and where your expertise lies.

CREATING A WEBSITE

Creating a website is not difficult and mainly involves two steps: 1) buying any necessary web addresses (URLs), and 2) having somewhere to host your content. If you want to think of building a website like building a house, these two steps equate to 1) having a location for your home, and 2) owning the land on which your house will be built.

There are dozens of websites you could visit to create a website, but I lack the time to evaluate the pros and cons of each. My first piece of advice is to seek out a savvy friend or relative who can help you. Since your website will be fairly simple and you'll be creating all the text yourself, asking for some help is not a huge favor to request of your niece or that one guy at the gym who works in computer software.

That said, if you have nowhere to turn to, just use WordPress[2]—simple software that will guide you through creating a website or blog or both. Wordpress.com will allow you to set up a simple, free blog. It has hundreds of different layouts (appearances) that you can use as your base template. In other words, you pick how the site looks. For a yearly fee, you can choose a unique URL (web address). From there, you can change lots of functionality, set your pages, provide your web page copy,

---

[1] If you're still confused about this, visit my sites to see the difference. Note how chucksambuchino.com is a static website, whereas guidetoliteraryagents.com/blog is a fluid blog that's updated every day.

[2] To learn a little more about the different functions of WordPress, visit en.support.wordpress.com/com-vs-org

and much more. If WordPress is not for you, Bluehost.com is another popular and simple one-stop location where you can buy a website, have somewhere to put the information, and pick a custom URL.

INVEST IN URLS

When considering the best URL for your home website, the commonsense option is to make it your full name—in my case, chucksambuchino.com. Purchasing a web address can run you anywhere from $10 to $40 per year per URL. When you buy your name, the Internet domain registrar (such as Bluehost.com or GoDaddy.com) cuts you a deal if you purchase multiple addresses.

ELEMENTS OF A GOOD WEBSITE

Here are the elements I consider mandatory for any writer website. These will be your foundation.

- **LANDING PAGE.** What is the home page of your site? Typically writers either have a "Welcome" page that points out all the different pages/aspects of the site, or the landing page is the writer's blog, so the first thing visitors see is the most recent news/post.
- **"ABOUT ME"** page. This is your chance to explain who you are and what you do. I would advise you to keep your bio length comparable to your accomplishments. If you're just starting out, then your bio should be somewhat short, naturally. Telling us a long story about how you've loved to write forever (almost all other writers have, too) will do you little good. This "About Me" page should include a head shot. And whether or not your social media links (Twitter, LinkedIn, and others) are on your home page, feel free to list them again here.

- **"MY BOOKS" OR "PORTFOLIO" OR "MY WRITING" PAGE.** Tell a little about what you're writing. Once again, I would expect the length of this page to be in direct correlation to your accomplishments. If you've published books, this is where you post the covers and links so writers can buy the books. If you've written magazine articles, this is where you would list your credits and even scan some articles online so people can see professional clippings. Lastly, if you have yet to be published, this is where you can talk generally about your own writing, such as how you are "currently writing a guide on how to lose weight by swimming."
- **"CONTACT ME" PAGE.** This is crucial, as making yourself easy to contact is one of the fundamental principles of platform and one of the best reasons to start a website in the first place. Provide an e-mail address or some kind of contact form that you check frequently.

MORE POSSIBLE ELEMENTS FOR A WEBSITE

Here are the elements I would consider optional for any writer website. These aspects, if you choose them, will take your site to the next level.

- **"BLOG" OR "NEWS" PAGE.** If your website home page is a true landing page ("Welcome!"), then you may want to have your blog on another page, or at least dedicate a separate page to news. This will allow you to have a page of your website that readers expect to be in flux and updated with new content. After all, if you're promoting an upcoming online class that you're teaching, where will news of that announcement fall on your site? If there is no logical place for it, you might be tempted *not* to post news of it, which hurts your platform.
- **"RESOURCES" PAGE.** If you're truly building a community, you will have come across great resources (other websites of note) online. The most common form of sharing resources with your readers is a blogroll, where you list a number of blogs that you find useful. A resources page can link to blogs or just

other helpful sites within your niche. (Make sure that when you create the links, you have them open in a new window, so readers aren't leaving your page completely.)

- **"EVENTS AND SPEAKING" OR "WHERE I'LL BE" PAGE.** If you're going to be signing books somewhere soon or an interview you recorded will soon be on television, I say, "scream it from the mountaintops." List everywhere you're going to be and don't spare the details. Give out addresses, links to more information, the time of the event, whether it's free or not, and any other incentive for people to show up. This page, much like your testimonials page, not only serves a purpose to your platform, but also ups your credibility. Remember to include a note on the page that says you're open to becoming a prospective speaker/panelist/interviewee ("Just e-mail me to discuss details… ").

- **"FIND ME ONLINE" PAGE.** If you are trying to direct people to other social networks (your Twitter, your Facebook, your blog, your groups) and haven't done it on your home page or bio page, simply create an entire page dedicated to where you can be found online. If you're spread all over the place through platform planks, this page is an important step.

- **"REVIEWS" OR "TESTIMONIALS" OR "INTERVIEWS" PAGE.** You can name this page whatever you like, but the purpose of it is to essentially toot your own horn to some degree. You can post excellent reviews of your books, testimonials about your services, a list of awards you've won, or a combination of all of these. The goal of this page is to instantly up your credibility and prove you're an established and accomplished professional who is worth knowing and following. Feel free to also link to any interviews you've done online.

- **"SERVICES" PAGE.** If you offer freelance services of any kind (editing, consultations), say so here. Only share what you want to share. For example, on my site I explain exactly what I edit, but I don't mention money. That is a personal discussion between myself and a possible client.

/IMPLE I/ NOT BAD

Your site doesn't have to rival the fancy look of the latest block-buster film's website. Simple is by no means a bad thing. For me, my chucksambuchino.com website is simply a landing page, so its simplicity serves its purpose just fine. Furthermore, your site should have no issues working on any kind of Internet browser (Firefox, Explorer, Safari, or others) or any mobile devices. Websites that require a lot of time to open (those with an intro or Flash) will not work well with older computers and/or some cell phones. I suggest testing how your site operates from a variety of devices and browsers.

YOUR HEAD /HOT AND BIO

Your Head Shot

If you don't have a professional photo or head shot, I suggest you get one taken by a professional photographer as soon as possible. You'll need it for your website and interviews and lots of other places—and sooner is better for having it done because you ain't getting any younger. Don't underestimate the value of a nice image, because appearance matters more than we'd like to believe. I was at BookExpo America in 2008 when I ran into the great literary agent who gained fame by blogging anonymously as "Miss Snark" (misssnark.blogspot.com). She pointed across the expo floor at a client of hers. Struck by the client's beauty, I told Miss Snark that her writer was definitely a looker. "Yeah," Miss Snark said, smiling. "That's what we like to call *platform*." So don't skimp on a good head shot. Invest in yourself. Also, when people can put a face with a name, it helps them remember you. It makes you re-latable (Fundamental Principle #10).

If you're writing something unusual or offbeat—perhaps a humor book or quirky title—having a silly head shot around as a second option is not a terrible idea. "A goofy author photo helps," says Ethan Gilsdorf, author of the memoir *Fantasy Freaks and Gaming Geeks*. "I have a few with me dressed in chain mail, wielding a sword. If an editor looking for an event to feature sees your silly or visually striking photo, they might choose your event over someone else."

Your Bio

Take some time composing your bio. You want to get the maximum impact with the minimum number of words, and you should feel free to change your bio depending on where it's posted or who requests it. Consider my Twitter bio, which is limited to 140 characters or fewer:

> I help writers get published. I edit the *Guide to Literary Agents,* and am the author of *How to Survive a Garden Gnome Attack.* I love to play guitar & piano.

Immediately I convey an incentive: Follow me for information on getting published. Then I state my credentials quickly, mentioning that I am an editor and an author. Following that, I throw in a little something about myself to give the bio some personal flavor. For a broader example, let's look at how I recently trimmed my bio down in size and why I cut what I did. This was my original "long bio" that I passed around a few years ago.

> Chuck Sambuchino is an editor for Writer's Digest Books (an imprint of F+W Media). He is the editor of *Guide to Literary Agents.* He recently helmed the third edition of *Formatting & Submitting Your Manuscript* (2009). His humor book, *How to Survive a Garden Gnome Attack*, will be released with Ten Speed Press/Random House, in fall 2010.
>
> Chuck is a former staffer of several newspapers and magazines. During his time as a newspaper staffer, he won awards from the Kentucky Press Association and the Cincinnati Society of Professional Journalists. He is also a writer and freelance editor. He is a produced

playwright, with both original and commissioned works produced. He is a magazine freelancer, with articles appearing in *Watercolor Artist, Pennsylvania Magazine, Cincinnati Magazine,* and *New Mexico Magazine.* During the past decade, more than 700 of his articles have appeared in print.

His website—the Guide to Literary Agents Blog—receives more than 115,000 page views each month. See it at www.guidetoliterary agents.com/blog. He is represented by Sorche Fairbank of Fairbank Literary.

Over the years, I've noticed that long bios can actually *hurt* you. The more things you sell/mention (i.e., the more you stuff into a small space), the thinner everything becomes. It was with that in mind that I went back to simplify my bio. Here is what I use now.

Chuck Sambuchino is the editor of *Guide to Literary Agents* and *Children's Writer's & Illustrator's Market* (both Writer's Digest Books). He is also the author of the writing books *Formatting & Submitting Your Manuscript,* 3rd ed. (2009) as well as *Create Your Writer Platform* (2012). He runs the Guide to Literary Agents Blog (guidetoliteraryagents.com/blog), one of the biggest blogs in publishing.

Chuck is a humor book author. The film rights of his 2010 book, *How to Survive a Garden Gnome Attack,* were optioned by Sony. His next humor book is *Red Dog/Blue Dog* (reddog-bluedog.com; 2012). Besides that, he is a husband, cover band guitarist, freelance editor, chocolate chip cookie addict, and owner of a flabby-yet-lovable dog named Graham.

Here's what I did to focus my bio in a shorter, better version:

- I divided it into two clear parts—"work Chuck" and "writer/personal Chuck." I want people to know I can 1) help them get published, and 2) make them laugh.
- I cut out all my journalism and playwriting credits. When I show up at conferences, I am not trying to solicit freelance article assignments or stage play rewrites, so there is little point in mentioning this.

- I mentioned my agent and blog page views early on because I felt like I needed to prove myself. Now I feel like the brand and published books convey enough authority.

The edits helped me cut my bio down in size by 30 percent, and they also helped me focus it on what I want the reader to take away. If you're frustrated because your bio lacks anything influential or impressive at this point, I urge you to simply *breathe*. Your bio will grow. Include anything you can that has to do with your niche and platform, and build as you go. Don't exaggerate your accomplishments—doing so will only result in people mistrusting you later.

WEBSITE MENTIONS IN YOUR QUERY LETTER

If a query says, "Learn about me at my website," is that a total turnoff? In other words, do you want platform and bio specifics up front in an author's contact with you (such as in a query letter)?

"I would expect an author to include important biographical details and platform specifics in a query, but it's always nice to include a link back to his or her website. If someone only included the link, however, it would definitely be frowned upon (it seems really lazy to me to require a perspective agent, who is rooting through hundreds of queries, to hunt around for pertinent information about a potential client rather than provide it for them outright in the query)."

—**ALYSSA REUBEN** (*Paradigm Literary*)

"I would rather you tell me everything I need to know to make a decision about you and your project up front in your query and then offer me your website address for more info if I'm interested beyond the initial introductory information. Make it as simple as possible for me to think, 'This is something that's intriguing!' and don't make me leave the page for that to happen. If you've done a good job on the query, I'll likely want to see more, so certainly nothing's lost in giving the website address after that."

—**GINA PANETTIERI** (*Talcott Notch Literary Services*)

"I absolutely want these specifics in the query, but if the author has included their URL in their letter (often this will follow their closing/signature, if it does not appear elsewhere) I will usually click on it and take a quick look. I don't think the author should take it for granted that an agent will go even that far (click on a provided link), so they should not use this as a shortcut. The letter itself is important—how the author expresses her- or himself."

—**STEPHANY EVANS** (*FinePrint Literary Management*)

"I like to follow a link further *if* I am incredibly captivated by the query. So include all of the relevant information in your query and entice me to want to learn more by clicking through to your website."

—**BERNADETTE BAKER-BAUGHMAN** (*Victoria Sanders & Associates*)

"I want some specifics in the query. The book flap won't say 'Learn about me at my website.' The query shouldn't either."

—**LAURIE ABKEMEIER** (*DeFiore and Company*)

"I am completely turned off by this. When queried by a writer, I expect them to provide me with all relevant bio and platform information up front."

—**SHAWNA MOREY** (*Folio Literary Management*)

CHAPTER 8

YOUR BLOG: THE EXTENſION

When you build your website (see Chapter 7), the site and pages you create will remain mostly static. You'll spend a lot of time putting the site together, making it look good, and ensuring that everything functions properly, with your search terms ("Cajun Chef," "prolific speaker") appearing how and where you want them to. But after that, you'll just be making minor updates and adjustments over time. You will shape different pages for their own specific purpose and rarely update it in any drastic way. That's it.

A *blog*, on the other hand, is an opportunity for you to constantly provide information on a scheduled basis. There is no limit to the information you provide or the length of each post. It's very common for a blog to be one section of a writer's website—the "in flux" page that is constantly relaying news, updates, and valuable new content.

WHAT IſA BLOG?

The word *blog* is short for *weblog*. Literally, it's a web log: a log of happenings found on the web (Internet). Imagine it like this: Let's say you went to Italy for a year and chronicled all your destinations and fun times in a journal. Now let's say that instead of the journal being something physical that you carried around, it was actually online, available for all to see and enjoy, and you uploaded chapters with the click of a button. *That's* a blog: a living, fluid website that's updated on a timely basis, be that once a week or once every few hours.

A blog is your optimal location to post large amounts of content. After all, you can't post a 500-word essay on Twitter, Facebook, or LinkedIn. What will drive followers to you is good content, and a blog is one of the easiest and most logical places to provide oodles of information.

BLOG EXAMPLEƧ

If you're completely new to the blogging arena and still don't understand what a blog is or the kinds of content they provide, look over these examples to get a quick and easy taste.

1. PoliticalWire.com (politics)
2. SlashFilm.com (film/movies)
3. PerezHilton.com (celebrity/gossip)
4. CakeWrecks.com (humor)

WHAT'Ƨ THE PURPOƧE OF A BLOG?

At its most basic level, the purpose of a blog is to give away content for free on a regular basis in an effort to build a steady and significant readership. As this readership begins to form (and your platform grows), you can turn this momentum into financial success, either by selling products and/or selling yourself as an expert in your field. And, naturally, one of the things you can sell to readers is a book. That's why, if you create a successful blog, you will have created a legitimate avenue to sell books to people who will buy them from you. At that point, you're ready to approach agents with a proposal because you can prove to them that a market exists for your writing and that a publisher will make money by publishing your book(s).

A great blog will be one of your key resources in building a community and brand. You will provide people with free, quality information—hopefully it's information that they can't find elsewhere or at least they can't find it easily. But at the same time, resist putting *everything* online. If all your content is free on the Internet, then there is little motivation to buy your works or solicit you for a paid speech.

HOW DO YOU CREATE A BLOG?

The good news about creating a blog is that starting one is free. Several websites will allow you to create a blog at no charge, and you can pick your choice of a simple design. These sites include the following:

- WordPress.com
- Blogger.com
- Tumblr.com

Starting a free blog is easy as pie. The great thing about constructing things like a WordPress website or any kind of blog is that instructions are abundant online. Countless people have had the same questions you will soon have, and all kinds of forums and answer boards tackle almost any problem you can come across.

Keep in mind that you don't want to just create a blog. You want to create a blog and a website. If your blog is *part* of your website (one of the main pages or the home page), you likely don't need an entirely separate blog from a site like Blogger. Your main website can take care of both, if you wish it to.

> "I use Blogger for my personal humor blog (the lifeofdad.com) and WordPress for the Writer's Digest blogs (writersdigest.com). The key difference, in my opinion, is that Blogger is simpler and easier to use, whereas WordPress allows you to have more control."
>
> —**BRIAN A. KLEMS**, *author of* Oh Boy, You're Having a Girl *(Adams Media; spring 2013)*

SUCCESSFUL BLOGGING PRACTICES

What will separate the most trafficked sites from all the other thousands of competing blogs is simply quality and value. Read on to learn about basic good blogging practices that can be implemented, no matter your niche or site specifics.

CHOOSE YOUR NAME AND URL WISELY. You only get one shot at this, so choose your name wisely. Your blog URL (web address) can be very simple, such as chucksambuchino.com/blog or chucksambuchino. blogspot.com. It can also focus on your niche, if you choose—such as LiveCheaply.wordpress.com.

POST CONSISTENTLY. Try to set a consistent frequency for your posts, be that once every Monday to kick off a week or once every day. What I love about getting writing news from WriterUnboxed.com, for example, is that there is one new column posted every day, and guest columnists rotate in order. In other words, I know what I'm going to get, which is a reason I frequent the site.

CREATE POSTS THAT ARE OF VALUE TO READERS. This all comes back to Fundamental Principle #1: "It is in giving that you receive." You must define what can be considered of value to your target readers. To examine this, let's take a look at my work blog as an example. I asked myself, "What would be of value for writers who are trying to get an agent?" Some answers were obvious—announcements of new agents looking for writers, interviews of established agents, commonly misunderstood words defined. But what else was of value to writers? An answer I had ignored to that point was *free books*—so I started adding giveaways to most of my guest columns. Later, I added contests to the mix, further upping the site's value (and, in turn, its page views). The challenge for you will be to discover what your audience finds useful and create it for them.

AVOID POSTS THAT ARE TOO PERSONAL AND/OR BORING. To some degree, your blog will have some of *you* in it. You'll write online about your life and your journey and your successes and your challenges in either a big way (if you are the focus of the blog) or in a small way (if you want to inject a little personality from time to time). But you must never get lazy and start blogging about boring things—such as what you had for lunch or how weird it is that your mailman whistles as he works. Also, avoid any information that would be considered TMI (too much information), such as your love life conquests, how your dog is constipated, or how mad you are at your spouse because he ignored his chores this week. (Caveat: Naturally, if your niche is all about how to be better in the sack, then your niche forces you to make TMI an aspect of the blog. That's okay.)

UTILIZE BULLET POINTS, SUBHEADS, AND NUMBERS. An easy and effective strategy concerning blog post titles is to use numbers, such as "7 Things I Learned So Far" or "5 Tips for Writing a Novel Synopsis." A simple glance through this book reveals many instances of this approach—especially with sidebars. Bloggers use numbered lists because readers love bite-size pieces of information that they can chew and digest. These pieces usually come from a numbered list, subheads, or bullet points that break down information and give readers jumping points—making the content easier to understand and breeze through.

USE LINKS IN YOUR POST. Link to other posts you've written or perhaps interesting columns you've found from around the Internet. If there is an option, allow clicking on the link to make a new tab or window open, so people don't leave your blog by going elsewhere. A mistake novice bloggers make is to not link to other "competing" blogs. But don't forget that your blog is isolated at first, and a smart way to alert other similar professionals of its existence is to link to them and give them page views. When they investigate where those hits are coming from, they'll find you and check out your site. Again, it's a matter of giving first and reaping the benefits later.

START A SERIES (OR SEVERAL) IF YOU CAN. People like to know what they're getting when they read a blog. You start by focusing on a niche and providing content around it. After that, try a series or two to continue providing expected content. For example, readers of my blog will know that every week they will see a "New Agent Alert." Also once a week, I usually try to add installments (guest columns) for other recurring series like "How I Got My Agent" and "Successful Queries."

ENCOURAGE AND RESPOND TO COMMENTS. It isn't enough to have people find your websites. You want them to stay a while and get involved—to interact with you and other writers. Encourage comments by responding to those who do comment. Try ending some posts with an open-ended question to brew discussion. On a side note, remember to comment on other people's blogs as you're perusing the Internet. (Remember: Give first.) This will help you make friends and start to build a community with others. And when you do draw more people to your blog, ensure that they can comment very easily—hopefully without having to log into any account. Besides making yourself easy to find, you must make yourself easy to *engage*, as well.

HAVE A PLAN MOVING FORWARD. As you create posts, you will be thinking day by day or even week by week—but feel free to plan further out. For example, for months I slowly collected guest columns written by literary agents. This allowed me to go ahead with my plan of making an entire month "Agent Advice Month"—featuring 100 percent expertise from the mouths of agents themselves. I could not have made that month happen without looking ahead.

DON'T CREATE TOO MANY DIFFERENT SITES. If you just started four blogs (one on your dating life, one on pop culture, one on your love of noir movies, and one on indie pop music in San Francisco), then you have a rough road ahead. It will take too much time to develop all four, and you're likely spreading yourself too thin.

MAKE YOUR POSTS EASY ON THE EYES. Again, looks *matter*. Show your site to a few peers and friends to get some early feedback. Besides that, try these starting tips below when designing blog posts that are easy to read. (Note: A bulleted list!)

- Break up paragraphs of long text.
- Add white space wherever possible in a post by keeping paragraphs to a manageable length and allowing breaks and open space.
- Use images in all posts (they even help with your search results!).
- Use dark text on a light background (i.e., don't have white text on a black or purple or navy background because it's harder to read).

- Categorize/tag your content. After you write a post, create categories that define its subject matter, such as "business," "sports," "interview," or "New York City." As you continue to write posts, you'll create new categories and use the old categories over and over again. This allows readers to click on a category that takes them directly to that which interests them the most.

BLOG POSTS AND FREELANCE ARTICLES: NOT-SO-DISTANT COUSINS

A lot of the advice you see in this chapter on blogging translates nicely to contributing freelance articles to magazines, newspapers, and websites. Keep that in mind as you skim over this chapter's bigger points. Specifically, consider these similarities:

- Just as how-to columns and interviews make for good blog content, they also serve as great article ideas.
- Just as blog post titles that utilize numbers will catch readers' eyes, article titles that use numbers will do the same.
- The fundamental goals of content anywhere—to entertain, inform, influence, or educate—translate to article writing just as easily as they apply to blogging.

CREATING CONTENT

What kind of content or advice goes into an average blog post? Is it always some kind of column? Well, it certainly doesn't have to be. Below are some easy templates for post ideas. Just remember that no matter what you're blogging about the site must be for *readers*. The content must be for *them*, not you. Stick to that mandate—providing value for others above all (giving)—and everything else will fall into place.

- **A "HOW-TO" COLUMN.** How-to columns are a staple of most blogs. If you can teach readers something they want to know, you will win their hearts. Teach how to create a delicious red velvet cake, how to take advantage of iPhone shortcuts, how to save money on taxes—or just about anything else. With no doubt, how-to pieces can and probably will be a large segment of your posts. They can also be newsy and relevant, such as "4 Ways You Can Still Get Tickets to the Super Bowl" or "Where to Park Downtown For the Fireworks Celebration."

- **AN OPINION PIECE.** These types of posts are not fact based, but more about you asserting an entertaining or educated opinion about something—such as "The Best Science Fiction Movies of the 1980s" or "My Favorite Dog-Friendly Towns in Colorado." While not "fact," it's still quality content—and that will result in visitors and page views.

- **AN INTERVIEW.** Interviews work great on several levels. First of all, you're not really spending any time writing a post or creating content; the interviewee is doing that for you by passing along her answers. Second of all, by incorporating that person into your blog, your site will hopefully turn up when his or her name is Googled. You're getting easy content that you didn't have to compose from scratch, and you'll get more page views, as well. Win-win!

- **A CONTEST OR GIVEAWAY.** Hosting a contest is sexy for your site because you're likely bringing a judge and prize to the table. Memoirist Ethan Gilsdorf (see the author case studies) praises giveaways: "I was able to partner with companies that gave me free stuff to give out as prizes for contests and promotions. In my case, I contacted gaming companies, other authors, filmmakers, and the like, and asked if they had free stuff they could give me. In my case, this merchandize related to gaming and fantasy: cheap plastic stuff, trinkets, dice, autographed copies of books, T-shirts, posters, free DVDs, and more."

- **PRODUCT OR ENTERTAINMENT REVIEWS.** People want to spend their time and money wisely—so they count on critics, experts, and everyday impartial folks to tell them what movies to see, what razor to buy, or what recent novel is guaranteed to make their hearts race. You can provide that value for them by reviewing just about anything—but hopefully you'll focus on something within your niche and expertise.

- **A ROUNDUP.** These are a common feature of writer blogs, I've found. What writers will do is read a lot of different sites on their quest to educate themselves and meet new people. While they're traversing all those websites, a writer will take note of the best columns they saw that week, and then list those posts in a roundup every week. But that's just a random example. A roundup can be anything and can look to the future just as easily as it can look to the past—i.e., one can create a roundup of helpful health-related columns they came across during the past week as easily as they can create a roundup of upcoming writing retreats people should consider.

- **A PERSONAL ANECDOTE.** For all I know, your blog may be *nothing but* personal anecdotes—perhaps it's a site featuring funny travel stories you've had with your four sons. But if your blog is more serious (how-to, prediction, newsy), it's important to add a personal element in some way. Telling an amusing, interesting, or funny story about yourself is a very good option.

- **NEWS BRIEF OR ANNOUNCEMENT.** I'm a movie junkie, which is why I check the blog SlashFilm.com every day. That site is a great example of a blog that's 80 to 90 percent news briefs. They simply gather and report on all kinds of movie news that's happening right now, and they do it exceptionally well, gathering more information than any other movie blog. Blogs that exist to collect pertinent information from a variety of sources (through lots of research) and then share it with you in one central location are common. These sites don't even have to create any new content to get readers. Their value lies in collecting content from everywhere else and displaying it in a way (usually short posts) that people can process large amounts of news quickly and easily.

- **PREDICTION OF THE FUTURE.** I'm not talking Nostradamus stuff here—I'm talking posts like "Why the Tampa Bay Lightning Will Win the Stanley Cup Next Year" or "Why So-and-So Politician Will Run For President Next Year." Make a case for something in an educated way, and get your readers to believe in the reasoning behind your prediction.
- **ANSWERS TO READERS' QUESTIONS.** When I was struggling for blog content early on, I encouraged readers to e-mail me their questions about publishing. When I received a good question, I posted the answer as a featured Q&A. *Voilà*—easy content. And since others must have the same questions ("Do literary agents in the United Kingdom consider American writers?"), my content will hopefully turn up in Google searches.
- **EMBEDDED VIDEO OR AUDIO CONTENT.** You can serve your main goals—to inform, educate, entertain—no matter what media you're presenting through. To mix up the content on your blog, think about adding a podcast or video into your content to shake things up.

BLOG-TO-BOOK DEALS

Is it possible to get a book deal solely from a successful blog? It's difficult, but it's certainly been done before. A majority of the successes I've seen in this arena are in the humor book market. Titles such as *Fail Nation*, *Passive Aggressive Notes*, *People of Walmart*, *Awkward Family Photos*, and more were all blogs that took off in popularity—and soon led to book deals.

Realize that only blogs of enormous size can warrant a true blog-to-book deal. So if you're getting twenty thousand page views a month on your site about the Olympics, that alone will likely not be enough. (The humor sites that inspired the aforementioned books get hundreds of thousands of page views a month, if not higher numbers.)

You want to start blogging in support of your book project and gain a platform. It is very unlikely that your content will be picked up as is and pasted into a book. Keep that in mind when mapping out your book as well as your posts. Blogs that translate well into books are blogs with content that can be broken down into small pieces. Humorous photos accomplish this well. Blog-to-book deals such as *Rules for My Unborn Son* and *Stuff White People Like* also worked well because the content could stay sliced and diced from blog to book. Your book idea will more than likely be supported and supplemented by your blog.

HOW TO MAXIMIZE YOUR BLOG

Once you have your niche settled and your routine down, it's time to examine how to get maximum impact from your blog. Composing posts is just the beginning. Each post is its own mini marketing opportunity—here are easy ways to make sure each of your posts gets the most exposure it can.

ALLOW OTHERS TO SHARE YOUR WORK. Others may want to print out one of your blog columns and pass it around at a local writers' group. They may want to repost an entire post on their site. Heck, they may want to use one of your sentences as a quote in their senior yearbook. It doesn't matter. If they ask nicely, I would advise you say yes—provided 1) they give you full credit where they can and add your blog URL, if possible, and 2) their repurposing is small enough not to worry about hurting your chances of selling the material in a book.

ALERT READERS OF NEW POSTS THROUGH YOUR FACEBOOK AND TWITTER. So you've created blog posts—now what? Now you need to inform people that you have content to share. You do this by spreading the word through your other social media outlets—namely Twitter and Facebook. (When alerting readers through Twitter, convert your long webpage link—the URL—to a smaller link using a site such as tinyURL.com.)

ADD AN RSS FEED FOR E-MAIL UPDATES. Plenty of readers would rather get your content via e-mail automatically than have to check your site every day. Make sure you have an RSS feed option. This allows people to be notified by e-mail when you have posted new content of any kind (video, blog, podcast). Good choices to start with include FeedBurner and FeedBlitz.

TAKE TIME TO LEARN ABOUT SEO (SEARCH ENGINE OPTIMIZATION). When you plug a term or phrase into a search engine, why do certain sites come out as the top results? The answer: search engine optimization. Search engines such as Google are looking for different things when they stack the search results. This is a vast topic, and plenty of it can get technical if you really want to dig deep, but here are three quick tips to getting more page views through searches:

1. Make sure you have a clear, straightforward headline rather than something generic or a pun. If your post is all about how to change a tire, simply call it "How to Change a Tire." After all, isn't that exactly what people will search for when they need help? If you title your post as a pun—"Tired Days Are Here Again"—it's no surprise that people won't find it in a search.
2. Use keywords in your title, subheads, and text. If people want to attend a writing event, imagine what they will search for using Google: "writing conference," "writing event," "writing retreat," "writers conference." The terms are all similar yet slightly different, so try to use as many as you can in your text.
3. Have phrases or words in your article link to other pages. Use links to your own past notable content as well as other sites that are both large and similar in nature.

PAY ATTENTION TO WHICH POSTS ARE BRINGING PEOPLE TO YOU. Previously, I mentioned how a blog counter (such as Google Analytics—google.com/analytics) will help you quantify your blog (Fundamental

Principle #12) so you know how many page views you're getting. But bean-counting sites like these can usually also point out your most popular posts and show you what search terms people use to find you. This kind of information is extremely valuable, because it shows what kind of content is most effective to create. Example: I interview lots of literary agents for a series on my GLA Blog. After I had dozens racked up in the archives, I looked into the stats and found that some were getting many more page views than others.

I was getting lots of hits for interviews when the agents involved did *not* have a professional agency website. Since the agents didn't have sites, writers were piecing together information through whatever turned up in searches—and this made my interviews important. Upon learning this, I immediately went to my freelancers who conducted agent interviews and told them to focus on agents who didn't have websites.

HAVE LINKS AT THE END OF EACH POST FOR RELATED READING. If someone is reading your latest post called "How to Price Your Watercolor Paintings," they obviously have some interest in the subject matter—so guide them to related content on your site to collect more page views. At the end of each post, point out past posts that have similar subject matter and link to those pages. The goal is to have a visitor bounce from post to post on your site.

GO BACK AND OPTIMIZE OLD POSTS. When you're several months into blogging and are starting to get the hang of what works, you're going to notice how messy your old posts are. When you have blogging downtime, look through past posts and improve them. If there's no image, add one. If there are no links at the end, include some. If you think a column could be even better with a simple sidebar, add it.

RECYCLE OLD POSTS. There's a very good possibility that some of your early blog writing is excellent but virtually no eyes saw it because your site had little traffic. So feel free to recycle and reuse that content. You can repost the content at the top of your blog again (I did this several times and called it a new series named "Blast From the Past"), or you can use a column as content for a guest post on another site. Don't be afraid to reuse content as an unpaid guest column for another site, and don't be afraid, when you're offered, to take someone's reprinted material as a guest column on your own site. It all adds up.

OCCASIONALLY REQUIRE PROMOTION FROM READERS. Most content I create online is easy to provide, in the grand scheme of things. But when I host a contest every now and again, I spend a *lot* of time putting it together. And since the contest is such a special post, I require participants to do something for me in exchange for entering. Typical requests include the following: 1) spreading the word via social media one or multiple times, 2) liking a page on Facebook, 3) signing up for the blog's RSS feed. If your prize/contest is worthwhile, people will do as you request. They will promote your blog *for* you, and help build your platform.

MAKE YOUR MOST POPULAR POSTS EASY TO ACCESS. If it's possible and you have some impressive posts to share, think about listing your "greatest hits" down the side of your blog. That way, new visitors can easily move through your best content and quickly see you're an expert with great information who should be followed online.

PROVIDE AND ACCEPT GUEST CONTENT

Remember Fundamental Principle #2: "You don't have to go it alone." Blogging provides an excellent opportunity for you to work with others and find success through collaboration. My own blog numbers grew drastically after I started reaching out to novelists for guest posts. They needed ways to promote their books, and I wanted awesome daily content. It was a natural fit, and all parties were more successful at the end of the day because of it. And do you know what the best part about this tipping point was? I work less! It's true. Now instead of creating several columns a week from scratch (a difficult endeavor), others create them for me: I just format them on my site, make them look pretty, and promote through Twitter.

Don't get me wrong. Before I could reach out to novelists and entice them to write for me, I had to build a solid foundation of readers, and that took one year of serious daily blogging (after a first year of not-so-serious blogging). But now that the structure is built, it's possible for others to do most of the work for me—and thus my blog has transitioned to autopilot (Fundamental Principle #6).

Also, just as I actively look for and solicit guest content for my own blog, I look for places where I can guest post when I've got something to promote—and I always give away a free book to a random commenter to generate more attention (Fundamental Principle #1).

HOW TO WRITE EFFECTIVE BLOG POST HEADLINES

Sidebar provided by Robert Lee Brewer (robertleebrewer. blogspot.com), editor of Writer's Market *and* Poet's Market.

1. Consider your main idea. Each post should have a main idea or point. If you have several main ideas or points, you probably have several blog posts. Break them up. Your headline should communicate your main idea or point.
2. Think keywords. There's a great free tool, Google Adwords Keyword Tool, for figuring out good keywords to include in your posts. Enter your possible headline and see if people are searching for it. The best titles have high monthly searches with low competition. But sometimes you're not going to get great results—because of the topic—so just do the best you can.
3. Think short. When you're creating that killer blog post title, keep it short. Experts suggest the first five words are the most important.
4. Spend time on the headline. Don't just dash off the first or second headline that pops into your head. Spend at least five minutes thinking about the blog post title. It could mean the difference between whether people read your post or not.

4 WAYS TO LURE PEOPLE TO YOUR BLOG

Sidebar provided by Alexis Grant (alexisgrant.com), writer and social media and platform coach.

Whenever I start following someone on Twitter and get an e-mail that asks me to check out his or her blog, I automatically delete it. Yup, that's right. A big, fat *delete*. Why? Because you shouldn't tell me to check out your blog—you should *lure* me there.

When a person tells me—or even asks me—to check out his blog, it feels forced. It makes him look like he's desperate for readers. The bottom line is, no one wants to check out a writer's blog just because it helps the writer. They want to check it out if it helps them. So how do you lure someone to your blog or Twitter feed or wherever you want *them* to go? A few ideas:

1. Make yourself look interesting. This is by far the best way to lure people to your site. Who doesn't love discovering bloggers they can relate to? Make yourself interesting, and people will follow you to the ends of the earth. Just answer this: What will readers find on your blog that will help them get where they want to be?
2. Make it easy to get there. Post the links to all of your social media channels prominently on your blog.
3. Add links to your e-mail signature. This is a subtle, not-in-your-face way of telling people you interact with where they can find you.
4. Interact. On Twitter, @reply or RT the person you want to notice you. Play the same notice-me game on Facebook by tagging pages. Or simply write the person an e-mail asking a question about their business or offering to help them.

CHAPTER 9

YOUR NEWJLETTER: THE OUTREACH

I would bet money that everyone reading this book receives newsletters over e-mail. The only real question is: *How many?* While I consider some things mandatory in building a platform (website, some type of social media), creating an e-mail newsletter is optional, but if done well, can be a highly effective tool. That's why people so often sign up for them and receive them.

An e-mail newsletter is a way for you to not only create content, but to deliver it straight to your community members so they do not have to remember to click through to your blog every day/week. It's easy for readers, and it allows you to stay on their radar and keep your visibility high.

The effectiveness of a large newsletter is indisputable. Of all the Writer's Digest marketing (platform) tools we possess—and that includes our blogs, almost 300,000 Twitter followers, Facebook, and the magazine—the number one selling tool for years has been our newsletter. Collecting e-mail addresses is key because you can directly reach those readers over and over again, easily, and the list of subscribers remains yours no matter what you do. It won't evaporate if you switch jobs or write a new book. Those followers are with you for the long term, and your list will only get bigger as time goes on.

Newsletters have a set frequency (weekly, monthly, etc.) and are just another easy way for you to provide content and build readers. Having a newsletter also offers you another leg of your platform that is instantly quantifiable. You can quickly deduce not only how many subscribers you have (an important number *agents* will want to know), but also how many people are opening your newsletter, clicking on your links, or unsubscribing (important numbers *you* will want to know).

STARTING YOUR E-NEWSLETTER

When you're ready to start an e-newsletter, make it professional. Don't bunch up fifty contacts at a time into Hotmail blasts and tell them news. Explore different options, and seek referrals from wise contacts who are already having success in this arena. For expertise on the subject, I spoke with the founders of WriterUnboxed.com, who started a newsletter in 2012 after five-plus years of blogging success. They chose MadMimi.com as a newsletter provider. The cost is dependent on how many people are on a list, so Writer Unboxed chose the $36/month option that allows up to ten thousand subscribers.

Another newsletter option is MailChimp.com, which (as of the writing of this book) allows you to start a free account with fewer than two thousand names, though there is a limit to how many total e-mails you can send each month. Here are some popular newsletter provider options:

- ConstantContact.com
- VerticalResponse.com
- Benchmarkemail.com
- GetResponse.com
- AWeber.com

Don't shy away from spending a little money for a professional service. I think writers get spoiled because they are used to little to no overhead with writing—but you shouldn't avoid investing in your career where need be. The good news is that most newsletter services provide you with simple, effective templates that are easy to use, learn, and maximize.

Comparison shop. You will likely be paying for a service, so ask the newsletter provider questions. Do you have to sign a yearly contract? What percentage of their e-mails regularly gets caught in spam filters and never reaches their intended recipients? Touching base will also let them teach you things you need to know. Also note: Do not overwhelm your readers. Send your newsletter monthly, or at the most, weekly.

FINDING CONTENT

Newsletter content can be original but does not have to be. It can be a mixture of published blog posts and reprinted material from guest contributors. Think of it as your "greatest hits" since the last newsletter. The typical first subhead in a newsletter, though not mandatory by any means, is a "Letter From the Editor" or "From the Editor" section. This allows you to forge a personal connection with readers.

At first, you will want your newsletter to be completely editorial content—i.e., no advertorial pieces or large sections where you hock your wares. As the months go on, I urge you to incorporate your products and events—so you can see some benefit from your platform. Depending on how many subheads (articles) your campaign has in each edition, you can make up to one-third of your sections about some kind of product or upcoming event. In other words, a percentage of your content can be used to promote *yourself*. If you don't feel comfortable mentioning yourself in a promotional sense through editorial content, you can create "ads"—notices or links that run down the side of the newsletter.

If you don't have a blog, then your content will be entirely original—thus making it more valuable but at the expense of other platform planks. The Writer's Market newsletter, for instance, is all original content. You can't find that instruction anywhere else, and *that* is the key incentive to subscribe. On the other hand, both the Writer's Digest and Guide to Literary Agents newsletters are mostly repurposed content that features either popular blog posts or news articles, or both.

Much like creating a blog, letting people know what to expect will help your cause. The first subhead of my own newsletter, almost always, is "New Agent to Query." Subscribers know that they can learn about at least one new agent every newsletter; they are familiar with my content. For my contributions to the Writer Unboxed newsletter, I've started the column "Ask Chuck"—a recurring Q&A section that tackles business questions about publishing.

What will your recurring content (series) entail? The sooner you start providing consistent features, the sooner your newsletter will have its own brand, and the more people will actually open and peruse your e-mail, rather than detailing it unread. And keep in mind, it won't matter if you have good content or not if subscribers aren't opening your e-mails—so make sure you have a catchy newsletter subject line that makes people want to know more.

"We created an e-newsletter because we wanted another way to connect the readers of our online community, and to offer unique insights and tidbits of news that we don't tap into on our main website for one reason or another. An e-newsletter gives us these options and allows us to directly reach a base of our most dedicated supporters. Having a focus helps fit all of the pieces of an initiative into place. When readers open your newsletter, they'll know what to expect because that's what you consistently deliver."

—**KATHLEEN BOLTON AND THERESE WALSH**, *founders of WriterUnboxed.com*

COLLECTING NEWSLETTER E-MAIL ADDRESSES

The major goal of a newsletter is to create a way for people to link with you and stay in touch with what you have to say (and sell). The more e-mail addresses you collect and more followers you have, the bigger your platform is and the more valuable you become as an author. Individuals would not be following you unless they were interested in you or your content—and anyone who is interested in you or your content will hopefully buy your services and products. "A robust e-mail list is especially attractive to publishers because we figure those are customers ready to buy!" says Beth Gissinger, former head of publicity for Adams Media.

To build your list of newsletter subscribers, start with these easy tips:

- Collect names before your newsletter goes live by inviting readers to give you their e-mail addresses. If your niche is established, people will begin signing up as soon as you make it easy to do so. When you release your initial blast later, remind subscribers that they signed up and your contact was indeed solicited.
- Simply ask your current subscribers and contributors to spread the word. If they root for you as much as hoped, they will mention your news. Make it easy for them to help by creating a tweet for them to share.
- Host a contest with a great prize, but stipulate that participants must encourage their own followers to sign up for your new newsletter by mentioning news of it on a social media site (such as Twitter).
- Find other up-and-coming newsletters with similar themes/content and have everyone promote everyone else at the end of each newsletter. Work together and rise together!
- Offer a free gift for simply signing up—such as a download, e-book PDF, or webcast you created.

- Constantly remind blog and website visitors to sign up by having notes on every page or friendly reminders at the end of posts/articles.

A temptation when creating an e-newsletter is to manually add e-mail addresses of people you know to your subscriber list. While not illegal, this method is *not* encouraged. If people want your newsletter, they will sign up for it. In fact, newsletter providers like MadMimi. com reserve the right to drop you from service if your newsletter features a high "unsubscribe" rate early on, as that implies that you have sent your newsletter to people who did not voluntarily opt in. It is also not encouraged to share your subscriber list without permission—i.e., selling e-mails to other businesses.

GETTING INVOLVED WITH OTHERS

If creating your own newsletter from scratch doesn't seem feasible, why not think back to Fundamental Principle #2 (work with others) and become a contributor or editor of an existing popular newsletter? In addition to running my own Guide to Literary Agents newsletter, I also contribute a column every month to the Writer Unboxed newsletter.

Let's examine this idea in action. Say you're an up-and-coming chef from the South who has a signature Southern style and wants to put together a book, but you have no visibility or name recognition outside of your hometown. You do some Googling and find large online groups for people who love innovative Southern cuisine. Members are a mix of cooks and foodies.

Here is my suggestion for moving forward: Join up to three organizations and get involved, even if they cost a small bit of money to join. Go to the largest organization first and express your interest in helping work on the group's e-newsletter for free. Offer to help edit it, interview other chefs, collect some simple news briefs—whatever they want. The specifics don't matter. Your goal is to get involved in the newsletter and earn your stripes in the group.

Now when you contact agents about your book, you have good visibility and can say so in your proposal ("I help edit the Southern Charm Cuisine newsletter, which reaches more than twenty thousand food lovers each month…"). By the time your book comes out in a year and a half, your position in the online group will hopefully have risen—but even if it hasn't, the newsletter will definitely give your book a healthy mention, hopefully many times over.

That's what a newsletter is there to do anyway—to report on news within an organization. If you're contributing to every newsletter, just make sure your quick bio or byline says "John Smith (johnsmith.com) is working on his first book, *The Creole Challenge Cookbook*," so that your hard work is paying off with constant small mentions of your book (either forthcoming or already published), which will be hyperlinked so people can quickly buy your work or at least see your website/blog.

CHAPTER 10

ARTICLE/COLUMN WRITING

Contributing articles, as a plank of platform, is not terribly far from blogging. When you freelance for magazines and websites, you're writing columns and articles that are read by large amounts of people. In other words, anyone can provide content on a blog, but only professionals can get paid money to compose content for large outlets—and that's the wonderful thing about article writing. Much like getting paid to speak, freelance writing for recognizable publications or websites will give you immediate credibility and hopefully lead to tipping points in your platform-building journey.

In addition to upping your credentials, adding names to your circle of media contacts, and putting money in your pocket, article writing also boosts your platform. With each article you write, your byline appears along with your website and/or your book titles. All of these things hopefully lead readers to your Internet presence (and books).

The upside to article writing is three-fold. First off, you are getting paid to write. Secondly, if you're freelancing for any kind of established publication or website, they already have a built-in audience. Your blog may still be growing, and if it's in its infantile stages, you may be frustrated about "speaking to nobody." However, if you write a recurring magazine column for a large regional website or national trade magazine, your work could easily be seen by tens of thousands of readers, if not more. Third, you're building editor contacts in the media. These editors are the decision makers who choose what books and stories to promote. If they *know* you, the chances of your book getting covered in their publication (or on their website) rise astronomically. Along with making money and building your credentials, you're now networking—and don't forget that who you know matters a lot in publishing, just like in any other business arena.

> "Ultimately, the book itself is still what matters most. That said, if a writer's bio can say they've written for mainstream publications known for great writing— the *New York Times*, *Outside*, Salon, *Slate*, *Atlantic Monthly*, *The New Yorker*, *O: The Oprah Magazine*, *Real Simple*, *Men's Health*—or even more specialized publications that are known for strong writing (*Bark*, for example), that's enough of a platform. If a writer can convey that she or he has media connections, has the writing chops to be accepted by the big boys, and is interesting, editors feel more confident [to buy his or her book]."
> —**LAURIE ABKEMEIER**, *literary agent, DeFiore and Company*

WRITING IN YOUR FIELD IS BEST

There are financial benefits to any kind of freelance writing, but your goal is more than money. Your goal is to write articles within your desired field of expertise (niche). When you do this, you speak directly to readers who will buy your books, and you also gain credibility and expertise as a speaker and author.

Let's examine how you can get platform through different types of freelance writing.

SCENARIO 1: You freelance for regional publications outside of your immediate area—as well as the occasional national trade magazine.

PLATFORM EVALUATION: This writing provides you with good credibility but little additional platform. The only way to have any success here is if the publication lists you at the beginning in some kind of "featured contributors" section where readers learn much more about some of the issue's writers (and their books).

SCENARIO 2: You freelance for regional publications in your area, such as the largest newspaper and a magazine devoted to life in the city.

PLATFORM EVALUATION: This is a smart way to go. When you contribute locally, you may be making a little less money than hoped, but you're getting in bed with the right people. From my own journey, I can tell you this: When my first humor book, *How to Survive a Garden Gnome Attack*, came out in fall 2010, I contacted all kinds of local media and asked them to cover the book. Only three outlets replied and gave me coverage. What did all three have in common? You guessed it. I wrote for them years before. The editors knew me and were much more likely to help me than other editors with whom I had no personal connection.

SCENARIO 3: You contribute free guest articles to large websites in your niche.

PLATFORM EVALUATION: This is also a smart way to go. You're getting your name, message, and byline on the websites your target customers frequent. Since you're writing for free, the logical trade-off is that your full bio appears with links to books on Amazon and even images of past titles, as well as your head shot. It's almost like you're providing content for free in exchange for an ad for your materials.

8 BASICS ABOUT FREELANCE ARTICLE WRITING

1. **SEEK OUT THE PUBLICATION'S WRITERS' GUIDELINES.** All publications have guidelines, which, simply put, are an explanation

of how writers should contact the publication in consideration of writing for them. Writers' guidelines usually address three key things: 1) what kind of pieces the publication is looking for (including length, tone, and subject matter), 2) how to submit your work for consideration (details on formatting and whether they accept e-mail or snail mail submissions), and 3) when and how they will respond to your request.

2. **YOU DO NOT HAVE TO WRITE FULL ARTICLES BEFORE YOU SELL THEM.** Selling a nonfiction article is exactly like selling a nonfiction book—you sell the item based on the concept and a "business plan" for it. Here's how it works: You compose a one-page query letter (typically submitted via e-mail) that details what the article/column will be about, as well as your credentials as an article writer. From that point, the publication, if interested, will contract you to write the article—and only at that point will you write it. Writing an article when no one has agreed to buy it is called writing on speculation ("on spec"). You can do this if you feel you need to, but you risk losing time on a project that may never see a financial return.

3. **CONSIDER WHAT THE GIG HAS TO OFFER.** Remember that in your case, the goal is *platform*. The goal is getting your name and work and bio in front of people who will buy your book and become followers. If an editor asks you to write a long piece for little money, that's not good. But are there benefits? Will you get more assignments in the future—and therefore more platform? Are you doing the editor a favor he will remember? Will writing the article put you in touch with key people you'd like to know?

4. **KEEP AN EYE OUT FOR NEW PUBLICATIONS.** New publications are actively seeking content to fill pages and are willing to work with newer and untested writers. I would suggest signing up to the following newsletters to get notices of any new publications or paying websites that pop up: *Writer Gazette, Absolute Write, Writer's Market,* and *Mr. Magazine.*

5. **WRITE FOR LOCAL PUBLICATIONS.** Besides the fact that you're be-friending local media pros who can help you later, you should know that local publications have a natural affinity for local writers. People always say "write what you know"—and you know your hometown and community better than anyone else.

6. **FEEL FREE TO AIM HIGH, BUT EXPECT TO START SMALL.** You'll have an easier time getting things published if you pitch shorter pieces and aim for small to midsized outlets. The goal is to *break in*, and then use your success and accomplishments to get bigger, better assignments. That's not to say you can't at least aim for *Real Simple* or The Huffington Post—just don't be surprised if they say no because you lack the experience. (But hey, it never hurts to ask.)

7. **YOU CAN RECYCLE IDEAS AND GET MULTIPLE PAYING JOBS.** One of the best parts about being a freelancer is your ability to re-cycle and reuse ideas. For example, I pitched *Ohio Magazine* a series that would profile historic theaters around the state that were still in operation today. After the magazine said no, I made a few changes to my query and sent it off to *Pennsylvania Magazine*. This time, the magazine said yes, and I got fourteen articles and paychecks out of it.

8. **READ THE PUBLICATIONS YOU'RE PITCHING.** Get familiar with several target markets and read back content, either online, with a subscription, or through issues at your local library. Note the tone of articles, the sections of the magazines, and the general feel of the magazine and its advertisers. From there, you will be better off pitching the best article ideas—and you will also find out if the idea you want to share has been used recently.

HOW TO COME UP WITH IDEAS

Hopefully, as you start to brainstorm, you will be coming up with ideas yourself. But if you need some prompts and avenues on generating ideas, consider these:

- **CAN YOU TAKE A LOCAL APPROACH TO A NATIONAL SUBJECT?** In these economic times, people are always looking for ways to spend less or earn more—so can you take a local approach to a national subject of interest (in this case, the economy)?

- **CAN YOU TAKE A NATIONAL APPROACH TO A LOCAL SUBJECT?** Perhaps you read something fascinating in a small local publication and want to see the topic examined on a nationwide scope. If so, go for it! Write that query. It was this very method of idea generation that got me my literary agent. She heard about my series on theaters for *Pennsylvania Magazine* and asked me if I had ever considered examining the subject on a national level for a book.

- **CAN YOU FOLLOW UP ON SOMETHING?** The *follow-up* is God's gift to writers. If you can't think of ideas, simply look at what's happened in the past and follow up on it. Look at what happened one, five, or ten years ago to generate ideas.

- **ARE YOU INSPIRED BY A STORY THAT ANOTHER PUBLICATION HAS WRITTEN?** If you're writing for local publications and websites, draw inspiration from other regional magazines. Simply go into a Barnes & Noble and start perusing other magazines that serve regional areas. Look at what features and columns are in those magazines, and see if you can take a similar approach for your local gigs.

HOW TO IDENTIFY POSSIBLE MARKETS FOR YOUR WORK

Once you have ideas, you need to figure out where to submit those pieces for publication. In other words, you will have to seek out markets for your work. Here are four easy places to find markets:

1. **WRITER'S MARKET OR WRITERSMARKET.COM.** If you sign up for the online subscription, you can search by subject keyword ("pets," "finance"). I myself got both *New Mexico Magazine* and *Pennsylvania Magazine* gigs by using this resource.

2. **AMAZON.** Go to Amazon.com and change the drop-down search to "magazines." Then search keywords regarding your niche areas ("science," "Orange County"). You'll find all kinds of publications you never knew existed.

3. **GOOGLE.** It's the best tool everyone overlooks. If you live in Atlanta, for instance, try Googling for local media outlets. Search "Atlanta magazine," "Atlanta parent news," "Atlanta women news," and lots more. You'll be amazed at what's right under your nose.

4. **BOOKSTORES.** Don't be afraid to simply go to the magazine section and flip through issues.

A NUMBERS GAME

Getting articles published is not easy—especially when you're new at it. There is heavy competition to get paid to write article-length work. Don't get discouraged if you get rejections because querying for articles truly is a numbers game. If a publication rejects you, re-query them with another idea, especially if the editor sent you a personal note.

"For every ten or fifteen pitches, I get one yes," says Ethan Gilsdorf, a contributor to national magazines and blogs. "Sometimes it takes several pitches to finally get an assignment from an editor. You have to be patient, resilient, consistent, and you have to keep pitching."

HOW TO CONTRIBUTE COLUMNS

Everyone wants to write a column (and that's why you should, too!)—but the intense competition for them makes it hard to land one. A column provides you recurring paid work and highlights not just your subject matter, but *you* as a writer with voice. *That's* platform. Chances are you'll get a head shot with each column and be able to include a nice bio. That's why a syndicated newspaper column is one of the holy grails of author visibility.

PITCH WITH A CLEAR TOPIC AND SOME FLESHED-OUT EXAMPLES. Make sure you have a well-thought-out plan before you start querying your ideas. Give the column a name ("The Garden Guru," "My Midlife Crisis") and a clear focus. Explain exactly what the column will be about. If you're already blogging on the same topic, point editors to some of your most successful posts—the ones with loads of comments. If your column concept is brand-new, then provide at least three fleshed-out examples of what the first columns will be like, and then add several more barebones concepts for column ideas. Make a case as to why readers of the publication will enjoy your work, and how this specialty column fills a subject void.

START SMALL. Community papers are great places to start. You could write for a local suburban weekly paper on how to enjoy an active retirement or anything else. If getting into print is vexing you, contribute to a local or growing website. The intent is to get paid for your work, but if the publication or site is big enough—and your end goal is to sell books—you might consider working for free (at least for a while).

USE YOUR SMALL SUCCESSES TO GET BETTER PLACEMENTS. Start by getting a column in a local paper, even if the money stinks. Insist that they put the columns online. (They will likely do this anyway.) With your columns online, you now have the important ability to *quantify* your success. You learn that you get ten thousand page views a month, and the number continues to grow. In fact, your column has become the most popular on the website. Success! Now take those numbers and notes and use them as ammunition to get a bigger gig. Using your small website success as a launching pad, approach a large metropolitan newspaper, and pitch your column.

COMMON PLATFORM MISTAKES

What mistakes do you see writers making in the construction of their platforms?

"The biggest mistake is waiting too long to get started. If a writer waits until his book is coming out, there will be a lot of ground to make up. Beyond that, I think putting an excessive amount of time and money into signings at brick-and-mortar bookstores and thinking that should be the basis of the platform will not give the return one hopes for. Most signings result in a very small number of sold books. You should view signings as an opportunity to establish relationships with the bookstore owners or managers. At the moment, I'm seeing book trailers as a waste of money. I'm seeing the people who would view them as people who are already fans and would buy your book anyway. Most of the ones being produced don't really grab the viewer and aren't distinctive or high quality enough to compel someone to want to read the book."

—**GINA PANETTIERI** (*Talcott Notch Literary Services*)

"My main concern is that you are utilizing the tools you have. If you are a blogger, is your readership growing? Are you effective in getting your message to your readers? If you are on Twitter for two years and still have thirty followers, it's not the right platform for you. Using social media badly is worse than not using it at all."

—**ROSEANNE WELLS** (*Marianne Strong Literary Agency*)

"Trying to do it all right off the bat is the biggest mistake I see. To start, authors should choose one or two platforms that they actually feel excited about (Facebook, Twitter, or blogging). Those are the platforms where you'll shine and gain a following that will then follow you over to your other platforms when your mean agent makes you start them."

—**MEREDITH BARNES** (*formerly of Lowenstein Associates, Inc.*)

"Oftentimes writers don't know exactly what to include in their tweets or blog posts. I've seen some authors use social media tools to air frustrations with publishers, editors, or their followers. Your brand is about your work and isn't something you want associated with negativity. It often helps to create a mission statement for your blog when you first get started so that you stay focused on your literary subject. Always keep in mind that consumers drive the market—stick to ideas that can help your readers."

—**REGINA BROOKS** (*Serendipity Literary Agency*)

CHAPTER 11

PUBLIC ƒPEAHING

In the movie *The Contender*, a high-ranking politician is asked why his opinion will be accepted by the masses of the American public without examination. His response: "Because I will have a very big microphone in front of me."

As I mentioned earlier, platform building often frustrates writers to the point that they bring up the term "catch-22"—pointing out that they need a book to get visibility, but can't get a book without visibility first. As you build your platform, you will be engaging in all directions, making small connections everywhere. However, in my opinion, very few avenues will give you more instant credibility than having some impressive public speaking gigs under your belt. Anybody can start a LinkedIn account. Anyone can write an op-ed for the local paper. Only professionals can educate a large group of listeners.

Your goals with public speaking will not be radically different from, say, blogging. You will do a lot of the work and outreach at the beginning, and gigs will start small with little money promised. But after you provide value and legitimately help people, then you'll acquire testimonials from contacts and organizers. You can use your initial success to get bigger and better speeches, and then use those as a résumé to land even better ones—and so on and so forth. Like any other avenue of writer platform, the core principles remain the same, and one thing indeed leads to another.

What makes public speaking very interesting is that to do it well, you must hone skills used in other areas, such as simple conversation and networking. Many public speaking venues exist, including radio interviews, TV interviews, podcast speeches, and webinar instruction. Most importantly, you're standing in front of people who may buy your book. That fact,that visibility, literally, is what will impress publishers.

TAILOR TO YOUR AUDIENCE

There's a scene in the movie *Sleepers* where a teenager in a juvenile detention center talks to a teacher. The class is studying *The Count of Monte Cristo* and the teenager offers the teacher a bit of advice on getting the attention of students in class. His tip: Skip to the part of the story where the main character escapes from prison. The message in this scene is simply to *tailor your speech to your audience*. Put yourself in their shoes and examine what they would want to learn and hear in a presentation. What will help and impress them? If you can help and impress them, they will come to you for more information. They will become a *follower*.

GIVE AN ENGAGING TALK

I know I sound like a broken record, but the key to securing speaking gigs is simply to provide *value* to those in the audience (Fundamental Principle #1). Said "value" can be a lot of things. You can inspire people. You can inform them. You can entertain them. When I give a keynote, my goal is to accomplish all three, and to always leave the audience with an air of enthusiasm.

In my opinion, the key to a good presentation, without question, is simply knowing your subject (and speech) inside and out. People who arrive completely prepared exude authority and confidence. Good speakers don't wing anything. They know exactly what information they want to provide and how to provide it. This is another good reason to develop a niche and become its go-to expert. The more you can appear to command a subject or topic, the more expertise you project. And the more expertise you project, the more people will buy your books.

LISTEN TO OTHERS AND LEARN FROM THEM. If you've never spoken before and want to start now, a good first step would be to see other good speakers in action. Thanks to sites like TED.com and YouTube, this is easy. Observe how other speakers operate. Pay attention to when you're most enraptured and when you couldn't care less.

USE ANECDOTES AND HUMOR. Anecdotes about yourself and others work because they take the lessons and themes of your speech and put them into real-life situations. Furthermore, when you use an anecdote you're not just telling your audience, you're *showing* them. We're back at Fundamental Principle #4—teaching people through examples, not just talk. Humor is key because it warms up the audience. Audience members are more apt to listen intently and buy books if they like the person speaking in front of them.

FOCUS YOUR SPEECH AROUND A SET NUMBER OF KEY POINTS. The truth is, people can't remember much of what you tell them. The audience's short attention span is a good reason to focus your speeches around a few key points. If your talk is something along the lines of "The Three Secrets to Launching a Successful Start-up," you immediately have several things going for you. If your speech will focus around three major points, this gives you three concrete areas to attack, and also concrete tips for the audience to take note of. Plus, if you're giving a brand-new speech that's not yet mastered—"Tax Information for Artists," for example—it behooves you to stay focused solely on a few key points. This allows you to feed listeners valuable information without touching on other areas you cannot speak to.

REMEMBER THAT SMALL VISUAL ELEMENTS ADD UP.

- Pay attention to your posture.

- Try to minimize stammers and "uhs."
- Do not fidget or constantly adjust the podium microphone.
- Make eye contact with the audience as much as possible. (A simple way to do this is to use a speech that's made up of major bullet points only. This forces you to not read word-for-word from the page, and it will allow you to look up when you talk.)

PUBLIC SPEAKING FOR NOVELISTS

Besides speaking on the craft and business of writing, novelists can seek out public speaking opportunities by doing public readings from their works. Another option is to speak on a main theme of your story (much like the "Loose Connection" niche in blogging). If your young adult novel features a bully, perhaps you can speak to students on antibullying initiatives.

If you do a public reading, don't charge anything for attendance—and think about getting a bigger attendance by sharing the event with a few other local (or similar) writers. Even better than reaching out to individuals is reaching to groups and organizations that share a common interest with you and your work. Make the whole thing an *event*—something that's not totally about you—to establish connections and meet important local professionals that would make good allies in promoting your book later. Plus, the more memorable the event, the more media publicity you're likely to receive.

LET YOUR SPEECHES EVOLVE

The beauty about composing an informative speech is that you can use it through various means—as a webinar script, a podcast talk, or a public speaking presentation. But no matter what platform avenue you choose, continue to constantly *refine* your talk as you go along. If you find a speech gaining and losing big sections of text over the years because of sweeping changes you employ, don't be surprised. You're simply responding to the audiences' reactions by tightening your message. Revise, refine, rephrase—repeat (Fundamental Principle #8).

With my own speeches, I find that a lot of their evolutions have to do with inquiries from the audience. I'm a fan of inviting the audience to ask questions for several reasons. First of all, doing so adds value to a speech. From an audience member's point of view, if he can ask you questions after the speech, he is not only receiving instruction, but also the chance to get a question answered should your speech not address it. When you open the floor to questions, your speech gains a new dimension, and so do you as a prospective presenter. Beyond that, audience questions provide a window into the concerns people are experiencing on their writing journeys, and I can include notes about their issues in future versions of my talk.

SPEECH LENGTH

Your best approach when composing a speech is to start with a long version. As you practice it aloud, you'll quickly discover which sections are lackluster versus those that shine. (Hint: In any speech, there are sections you enjoy giving and those you don't. This is your inner judge weighing on the strongest and weakest portions of your talk.) Once you have polished your long speech, you can easily customize it to fill the time specifications of any request. Conference leaders want a fifteen-minute talk? Fine. Thirty minutes? Also fine. In fact, there is an upside to giving a short speech. Whittling a long talk down to fifteen minutes means the final product will feature the finest fifteen minutes you've got, and the presentation will be dynamite, leaving the crowd wanting more. If you give a dynamite talk, rest assured members of the audience will want to learn more about you and your writing.

Also concerning time: Never go over your allotted time unless you have permission. Usually, someone will be scheduled to speak after you.

ALWAYS KEEP THE END GOALS IN MIND: PLATFORM AND BOOK SALES

While it can possibly make you money as you go along, public speaking is not a surefire way to take home a healthy paycheck. Rather, it's a means to establish your platform (and sell books, if you have some published). Never forget that. Building your platform and thinking toward the future should be your entire motivation for taking a day away from your family—so make sure your appearance and speech benefit you. Here are five tips for making sure your public speaking benefits you beyond the event itself.

1. **URGE AUDIENCE MEMBERS TO FOLLOW YOU ON TWITTER, BE-FRIEND YOU ON FACEBOOK, AND SIGN UP FOR YOUR NEWSLETTER.** The goal is for them to stay in touch with you for months and years to come. The more ways they can do that, the better off you'll be. If they fail to stay connected with you, how can they buy your book when it publishes next year? They can't! Keep in mind that people need motivation to stay in contact with you, so give them some. Here's how I will put it at a conference: "And if you're looking for a literary agent, I would highly urge you to check out my blog, sign up for my newsletter, and follow me on Twitter. All those channels include free information about queries, submissions, new agents, interviews, platform, and more. If you liked what you heard today, I've got plenty more that can help you on your journey, just as it has helped many others before you."

2. **MAKE YOURSELF EASY TO CONTACT IN ANY WAY POSSIBLE.** We're back to Fundamental Principle #5. When you speak at an event, pass out business cards. Have audience members write their e-mails on a sign-up list for your e-newsletter. If you provide handouts, include your Twitter handle and blog on the sheet itself at the top—and remind them what awaits them if they follow you ("For more information on getting an agent and building your platform, check out my blog…"). If you use PowerPoint to enhance your talk, have the final screen (the one that will ul-

timately stay up there the longest, during question and answer time) provide all the ways they can contact you and stay in touch.

"For me, it's become more helpful in terms of platform building to speak to organizations whose membership is comprised of my readers rather than my fellow writers. That means, given the subjects of my published books that deal quite a bit with women's empowerment, if I have to make a choice between a speaking engagement at a writers conference or let's say, The Women's Initiative on any given date, I'd choose the latter, because it stands to reason that a greater number of people who are interested in my particular writing would be in the second audience."

—**PATRICIA V. DAVIS**, *author of* Harlot's Sauce *and* The Diva Doctrine

3. **INFORM ATTENDEES THAT YOUR BOOKS ARE FOR SALE.** When I speak, I require that my books be ordered and sold at the events. The challenge, I find, is telling attendees they're available without coming off like a huckster. There is no easy way around this, so I usually just say it in a very matter-of-fact way: "Real quick, I wanted to say all my books are available at the event bookstore. [Explain the exact location of the bookstore, if necessary, and mention any specials or discounts the bookstore is offering.] Please feel free to check them out and see if they interest you. If you do get a book, remember to come find me because I will be honored to sign it. Thanks."

4. **AFTER A SPEECH, MEET PEOPLE AND ESTABLISH LASTING CONNECTIONS.** Providing your talk was an excellent one (and it will be), people will come up to shake your hand and ask questions

afterward. They're still buzzing from your talk. Why not ask everyone standing around if they want to grab dinner or drinks at a local restaurant? Make deeper connections with people who enjoyed what you had to say.

5. **FOLLOWING THE EVENT, ASK THE ORGANIZER FOR A TESTIMONIAL.** If you're relatively sure that they'll praise your skill, that testimonial is worth gold in terms of impressing other people who control event purse strings. In addition to politely requesting a testimonial, ask the organizer if they have suggestions for where else to speak.

JEEK GIGJ AND GET BOOKED

When you reach out to prospective organizers, it's of the utmost importance to have all your stuff wired tight. By that point, you should have a nice website telling all about you. You should have several prepared speeches with explanations of each. Hopefully you'll conjure up some speech topics over time (this comes naturally as you dive into a niche), but if you're having trouble, take this advice from public speaking expert and author Scott S. Smith: Google certain phrases and "speaker" and see what comes up. You could find some intriguing voids that you're able to fill. Perhaps your niche is Catholicism, and you Google "Speaker For How to Find Your Catholic Soul Mate." If nothing or little comes back with a direct match, fill that void by developing a speech and mentioning it on your website. Then you and your speech will turn up on the search engine lists.

On that note, when you create a website, make sure you write your speaking abilities/topics to turn up in searches. If speaking is a big part of your platform, have the word *speaker* high on your page, like in your blog header. And just as you want to develop helpful speeches in your niche, beware mentioning online or in person that you "can speak about anything." Comparatively, this is like writing a book "that anyone will enjoy"—and you know what they say about writing a book "for anyone." It means you're actually writing a book for *no one*. Specialize, specialize, specialize. The narrower your speech is, the less competition you have and the more value you possess.

"Start locally by approaching civic, community, and religious organizations. Develop a series of talks for your church or the rotary club and then move up to larger groups and venues. Ask everyone you know to help find bookings. Speak often and work your way up. Make your initial mistakes locally and build a devoted fan base close to home."

—RICK FRISHMAN AND ROBYN FREEDMAN SPIZMAN, *from their book* Author 101: Bestselling Secrets From Top Agents

START LOCAL AND BRANCH OUT. Local organizers like to work with local speakers. That's because nearby experts require little to no travel costs, and groups like to support local individuals. So start small and start local. Since you're a writer, maybe you can present on a writing topic at a nearby writers conference.

Beyond the category of writing instruction, your gigs will strictly depend on your niche, as well as what groups would be interested in hearing your expertise. Random examples:

- If you're writing a book about Alzheimer's or caregiving for those with Alzheimer's, look for a local chapter of the Alzheimer's Association
- Teaching—try a local chapter of the NEA or a teachers group
- Parenting—try the plethora of moms groups in your area (use Google)
- Business—try your local chamber of commerce
- Any niche—try offering free or low-cost classes/talks at local libraries, senior centers, community centers, and/or schools

- Any niche—look for conventions, trade shows, and national events taking place in town

And so forth and so on. Use Internet searches and ask associates to turn up interesting leads.

DON'T FORGET UNIVERSITIES, GRAD SCHOOL CLASSES, AND EDUCATION PROGRAMS. Classes and MFA programs always bring in guest speakers. Children's book writers and experts on education are always speaking at schools.

SPEAK FOR CHEAP, OR EVEN FREE, WHEN YOU BEGIN. What you charge to speak—from $50 to $5,000—depends on you, your niche, your expertise level, and how much you're in demand. Important note: If you're contacting *them*, you're not in a position of power to make negotiations. At first, *you* will be reaching out to organizations to get the ball rolling and will very likely speak for free/cheap. After all, remember the initial goal with platform development is to start small, build a foundation, and get balls rolling. Once you start to get busier with more bookings, word of your value will travel and top-tier organizers will cold contact you to teach. It is then—when *they* initiate contact with *you*—that you will have leverage with money requests.

RECOGNIZE THAT YOU CAN ALSO UTILIZE WEBINARS AND PODCASTS. You don't have to speak in person to build your public speaking platform. If you have a lot of information to share—perhaps your niche is sports, where new information is constant and abundant—then you might consider developing a podcast or a recurring video recap on your website.

DON'T BE UNGRATEFUL OR RUDE WHEN SAYING NO. If you broadcast yourself as a speaker, you never know who's going to contact you. If asked to fly across the country on your own dime to speak to five people in a living room, I'm guessing you'll say no. But when you decline an invitation of any kind, don't be brusque. Try to avoid saying, "Your event is of no worth to me because you can't pay my travel costs and speaking fee for being awesome. And now I must discontinue this reply—as I'm off to Dubai!" Politely say no; you might say that you have a scheduling conflict. If I decline a nonprofit group who's asked me to speak, for example, I'll do so very gently, then offer to promote their event in my newsletter and offer the coordinators of the event a few Writer's Digest books as door prizes, as well. The hope is to continue the goodwill between us (networking = platform), even though I couldn't participate as hoped.

4 FINAL TIPS ON PUBLIC SPEAKING

Please understand that because of limited space in this book, I cannot instruct you on things such as overcoming fear at the microphone or the perfect way to warm up your voice. But I do want to leave with four simple tips that have worked for me in terms of presenting well.

1. **GET ENOUGH REST.** I'll even take this one step further and tell you to go to bed early. That's because, the night before you do something important, it's very probable that you'll toss and turn in bed.

2. **JUDGE YOUR SPEECH ON EYE CONTACT AND SILENCE.** When you look around the room, how many eyes are on you? If people start to pull out their iPhones, you're doing something wrong.

3. **HAVE WATER NEARBY.** Your throat is going to get dry, so keep water close. The best time to sip water is after you make the audience laugh or when an attendee is asking a question. That way, drinking does not disrupt the flow of your talk.

4. **RECORD YOURSELF.** Significant value lies in recording your own talk and examining it later. My guess is that within two minutes of listening to a recording of yourself, you will pick up on at least one major thing you need to change—such as how fast you speak or the tone you use.

ſOCIAL MEDIA: TWITTER, FACEBOOK, AND MORE

Using social media to promote yourself and your expertise simply means connecting with other individuals through websites where people virtually gather. It's the evolution of networking in person to networking in a digital sense. The Internet has connected us all—and you should embrace connection possibilities if you want to increase your reach as an author. Social media gives us networking and reach that is beyond borders or limits. That's an exciting thought!

I'll share an embarrassing fact with you. When social media started its rise—especially Twitter—I was a big naysayer. It took me years to join up and get involved. "It'll never last!" I said. "What can anyone possibly say in 140 characters? It's preposterous, I tell you, *preposterous*!" And that's to say nothing of the fact that I was also the last of my friends to sign up for Facebook.

Well guess what? The joke was on me. Nowadays, I am in charge of the Writer's Digest webinar program, which relies on instructors that can spread the word effectively using their own platforms. The first thing I do to gauge a teacher's platform is, you guessed it, check their number of Twitter followers. What does that tell you about analyzing a person's worth in terms of platform? It means if you want to teach for Writer's Digest, the first thing I'm going to do is look up your blog and Twitter account, seeking impressive stats[1].

Want more evidence that the power of social networking is very real? During the summer of 2012, I saw the release of my second major humor book, *Red Dog/Blue Dog: When Pooches Get Political*. I can tell you without a doubt that the only reason that book came about is because of Twitter and Facebook. The book is essentially a large collection of photos that others submitted for inclusion. If I hadn't been able to spread my call for photo submissions and ask friends to do the same through their own networks, I would not have collected enough images to fill the book. It's absolutely true: Twitter saved that project. Flickr, a social networking hub for photographers, was also integral to getting the book published.

"The growth of the Internet has changed everything," says bestselling thriller writer Barry Eisler, in his interview on about.com. "Not so long ago, authors couldn't do much to promote themselves outside of the book tour and perhaps a few conferences or speaking engagements. The Internet, though, enables an author to promote continuously, and for obsessives like me, it's a pretty short jump from 'you can' to 'you must.' Now, I don't know anyone without a blog, Facebook page, and Twitter feed."

BEWARE BECOMING A "SELL MONSTER"

My former boss Jane Friedman once said that writers who joined Twitter because they just had a book released and were told to get on Twitter by a publicist ... *were too late*. In other words, it really helps a writer's cause when he can join groups and sites *before* he wishes to use channels to sell books. Otherwise the writer risks promoting his work too often or too forcefully.

---

[1] Again, what constitutes "impressive" will vary by category and judge. But to give you an example, I usually seek webinar instructors with at least 5,000 Twitter followers.

I've found that the best way to sell is by not directly selling. Build friendships and connect with people. "The quickest path to personal or professional growth is not in hyping yourself to others but in sharing yourself with them," says Dale Carnegie and the authors of *How to Win Friends & Influence People in the Digital Age*.

Take it from me, Barry Eisler, and countless others: Social networking is very real and very effective, but it can easily become a time suck if you let it. In this chapter, we will examine how to best leverage social media websites—specifically Twitter and Facebook—for maximum platform success.

Whatever you do, do not ignore new means to promote yourself through the Internet just because change seems daunting. If you want to sell a book, the first thing that gets judged under a microscope is your online presence. "In today's marketplace, the biggest emphasis in terms of author platform would be their online/digital platform," says Beth Gissinger, former publicity director for Adams Media. "How many followers do they have on Facebook and Twitter? What is their website traffic like, etc.? We really dig into these stats when deciding to take on a project."

Social media outreach allows you to easily do the following:

- Connect, network, and make friends
- Receive information/news and learn
- Share information that you created or found interesting
- Promote your work and the works of friends

While it's imperative that you engage in *some* kind of social media to build community and construct a platform, how you interact in these communities is entirely up to you. I myself am a the-more-the-merrier type of networker, while others have written open praise for minimalist approaches of interacting with fewer people but building only lasting connections. Like any other avenue of platform, remember to analyze and evaluate your progress (Fundamental Principle #8) so your efforts can evolve for the better.

Also important to keep in mind is that social media avenues can have limitations—such as the character restraints of Twitter. That's why you may want to use social media primarily as a way to optimize and augment your platform, while maintaining a base of operations to provide longer chunks of content—be that a blog, a website, or published columns. Social media is great, but your work in the arena needs to point people to great content. Otherwise any visibility you gain is for naught.

Working in social media also unveils another concern: Communicating is so effortless that you must resist the urge to share information that may put readers off. I find it disconcerting to read negative Facebook updates, tweets, and even blog posts that whine about this or that or complain about not having found success as quickly as the writer hoped. While self-deprecating humor is always appreciated (and even valuable, as it humanizes us—Fundamental Principle #10), straight-up whining will only slow your journey.

I want you to approach social networks slowly and with care. To make sure you're not wasting time or being ineffective, you should learn as much about any avenue of platform that you can before jumping in. This will save you time and hassles in the long run.

TWITTER

I want to start with Twitter (twitter.com) because I believe it to be, by far, the most effective social media network out there for writers. In my opinion, it's the most business savvy and fastest growing social media platform available, so joining up should be one of your first steps in your effort to market yourself. But don't just sign up and tweet without rhyme or reason. Twitter is a powerful new media tool, and that's all the more reason to use it with purpose and intent.

"A big mistake I see on Twitter is the I'm-talking-but-I'm-not-listening Twitter feed. Too many authors tweet without interacting. They retweet without commenting. They tweet nothing but links to their blog. It's not social media unless you're being *social*. Twitter is a total waste of your time and anyone who follows you if you're not following the three rules: Be useful, be personal, be interactive."

—**LAURIE ABKEMEIER**, *literary agent, DeFiore and Company*

The Basics

Twitter is a site that allows you to share small bits of information. By that, I mean each update you post (i.e., each time you speak) is limited to 140 characters. Using Twitter is different from virtually any other social media site because it severely limits the size of each contribution, forcing you to be concise and creative. Here are some quick facts you need to know:

- You can post (tweet) as much as you want.
- Your 140-character limit includes spaces, punctuation, and web links.
- Everyone's tweets are traditionally visible to everyone else. In other words, you do not have to be a person's "friend" (like Facebook) to see what that person is posting.
- Since you have space limitations, you'll want to share links by converting them to smaller URL links. Sites such as tinyURL.com do this for you.
- Your profile will be a "handle"—a name you choose preceded by the @ sign. The two Twitter handles I manage are a personal one (@chucksambuchino) and a business one (@WritersDigest). I suggest using something close to your real name and a real head shot of yourself, rather than getting cute.
- You can share pictures, but those images do not show up to readers immediately. Readers must click to another page to see pictures.
- You have the ability to privately direct message (DM) other users, but you must both follow each other before this tool is us-

able. To communicate with someone who is not following you, simply tweet them by putting their handle (@CBS, for example) at the front of your tweet.

Do not get overwhelmed by Twitter, or any other social media network for that matter. When you first begin, it's all naturally new and confusing, and the sheer amount of people on the site—combined with the amount of networking you *could* do should you choose to do it—can feel inundating. This will pass in a few weeks. You will soon feel more comfortable, and you will begin to experience some basic successes from your work (opportunities, new friends, a celebrity chitchatting you), which will give you much-needed adrenaline for your platform construction.

Common Tactics for Using Twitter

- **LEARN.** Before you really get going with tweets, I urge you to browse around and find dozens or even hundreds of people to follow. You can follow anyone from authors and literary agents to celebrities and comedians. Twitter's search function allows you to look for individuals, and the site will continuously suggest related individuals you may also want to follow. Once you're following plenty of people, you will see tons of information coming through your feed as all of your connections share interesting articles, content, and snippets. That's what makes the site an amazing educational tool. If you just sit and read the information that's coming through, you'll never stop learning.
- **SHARE YOUR OWN BLOG POSTS.** On your blog, you will have unlimited space to create posts about writing and any other content you like. Once you create a post, you must market that post by alerting people of its existence.
- **SHARE YOUR THOUGHTS.** Twitter is a wide-open network, so feel free to post what you're doing and thinking. Reading a great book? Say so. Just remember to mind your manners.
- **RETWEET OTHERS/SHARE.** If you see someone else's tweet and enjoy it enough to share it verbatim with your own followers,

simply "retweet" it (click on the retweet icon). Or if you find any kind of web page online that you'd like to share through Twitter, you can do so by manually converting the link to a smaller URL and sharing, or by seeing if the page has social media share buttons that allow you to share tweets quickly.

- **ENGAGE OTHERS.** If someone shares something you like, retweet it or send a note of thanks to that person. If someone's talking about something you enjoy, engage them. If someone asks a question to the masses looking for ideas, throw an answer her way. If you engage people, the hope is that they will befriend and follow you, thus adding to your network and platform.

- **CREATE LISTS.** You may very well follow a lot of people, and one easy way to parcel out all the tweets that come down is to assemble those you follow into lists. For example, if you're trying to get published, you can create a list solely comprised of literary agents. Another list can comprise friends and relatives.

- **SEARCH SUBJECTS OF INTEREST USING HASHTAGS.** Twitter users put hashtags before a word (#example) when they want their tweets to come up in searches and groupings. For example, whenever someone posts anything regarding our Writer's Digest Conference, we encourage them to end the tweet with #WDC. That way, anyone anywhere can simply search "#WDC" and turn up everyone's tweets from the conference in one collective grouping. If you search #knitting or #UCLAbasketball, you'll turn up countless people discussing those topics. Tweet with some of them and hope to make connections.

- **MENTION OTHERS USING THEIR HANDLES.** If your tweet is "Just had an amazing time at the philharmonic with Julie F and Jason B," then why not identify those people by their handles (@ writerJulez19 and @scififorlife4ever)? If you do that, both Julie and Jason will immediately see you've mentioned them, and they'll be happy to read your note.

- **GROW, LEARN, AND EVALUATE.** Once you get the hang of Twitter, consider using Hootsuite.com or a similar site to manage your tweets. Using Hootsuite allows you to tweet as usual, but you get more elements, such as the ability to schedule your tweets for the future as well as the ability to see everyone's retweets about you in the same Internet screen (rather than clicking somewhere else). Also, sites like Grader.com (and, to some degree, Klout.com) allow you to get a score on how effectively you're using Twitter.

MULTIPLE TWEETS?

Should you tweet the same thing more than once? Opinions vary on this. I'd have to guess most people do *not* post the same tweet multiple times, and one professional's reasoning against this was that Twitter is full of so much already, why clog up the mix even more?

All that said, I am a personal fan of multiple tweets. My reasoning is this: I estimate the average writer misses 90 to 99 percent of the tweets that go through their Twitter feed. That's an awfully big chance that people miss something I post. Therefore, if it is a business tweet (and not personal), I will post it anywhere from two to four times. All my new literary agent alerts, giveaway announcements, and news of writers conferences are posted many times. Obviously, I would never repeat a posting of how I just ate a delicious burrito or got my highest score ever on Tetris.

Twitter as a Business Tool

Perhaps more than any other social network, Twitter can be used as a tool of your platform and brand. You will tweet about book news and your blog posts. You will share industry news within your niche. You will attempt to connect with other business professionals.

Be sure to recognize that Twitter is an extension of your brand, so don't do anything that will damage it. If you are marketing to a writing crowd (like I am) it would not behoove me to use shorthand for fun (Whtz up 2nght?) or start posting a flood of articles about how my hometown city council members are bickering again. This information is of no value to my niche audience, and posting nonrelevant content will affect my perceived usefulness and authority.

> "Twitter is a way to make your brand personal. As writers, our name is our brand, so the key is to not only shape information but also connect with others. The more people you connect with in an open and honest way, the more people who will promote you when you need it. This will go a long way toward building your platform."
> —**BRIAN A. KLEMS,** *author of* Oh Boy, You're Having a Girl *(Adams Media, 2013)*

To build your brand further, reach out to people who share the same specialty—you might even send them the occasional tweet of your success here and there. Not only is it a common method of engaging industry professionals, I think it's a wise thing to do in an attempt to get on their radar. Ask them a question. Respond to their inquiries. If they're celebrating a New York Rangers victory and you love the Rangers, say something. Remember that your end goal with platform is to be visible to as many people as possible, and you and your books will not be noticed without effort.

Here are a few ways I've personally used Twitter to build my brand and platform and sell books on a weekly basis.

- I have saved searches for important keywords and phrases, so I can check daily who's discussing my books or me on Twitter. If someone bought a book of mine and tweets about it, I thank that person. If a person is discussing or recommending a book of mine, I'll engage them.

- Alongside many tweets, I sprinkle in news of conferences I'll be at. It lets people know about events they may want to attend and helps me spread the word about my speaking engagements. The more people that come to these events, the more audience members I can engage personally.
- I don't change my profile photo, and I have only once changed my bio. You don't build a brand by making drastic changes every month.

AVOID THE TIME-JUCK MONJTER

There is no end to how much work and promotion you can do through social media. That means you can spend sixteen hours of your day on the Internet connecting with people and still have more to do. It's this reason that you must ration your time online, before it becomes a time suck and takes away from more important projects such as writing. If you feel yourself struggling with this problem (and almost everyone does at some point), do two things: 1) limit your social media work each day—a maximum of one hour is good—and 2) evaluate, analyze, and evaluate again. Remember that it's okay to start small, but you should be seeing *some* growth in your efforts. If you're not, it might be time to switch gears, tactics, or messages.

FACEBOOK

Facebook (facebook.com) is the largest social networking site on the planet, so it's definitely wise to get on it as soon as possible. Unlike Twitter, which limits you to short bursts of words, Facebook allows you longer status updates, as well as the ability to embed videos, upload lots of pictures, and much more.

The Basics

Facebook is a social networking site that allows you to create a personal page for yourself that's all about who you are. Here are some quick facts you need to know:

- People sign up using their full professional names.
- You can only directly communicate with those who have confirmed that you are friends. People will search you out and ask for a friend request, and you will do the same to others.
- You can post status updates about whatever you like.
- You can include some basic biographical information about yourself, if you wish, and have it made visible to visitors, should you choose. This information includes your birthday, your alma maters, your current workplace, and your city of residence.
- You can post photos online and group them into folders.
- You can "like" and/or comment on the statuses, photos, and updates of any of your friends, just as they will do the same for your statuses, photos, and updates.
- Facebook has many different settings options—meaning you can change the page's accessibility to whatever degree you wish. For example, when someone you don't know pulls up your profile, your settings will allow that person to see a lot or a little, depending on your prefixed settings.
- When other people like or comment on your status, all your friends can see the discussion.

More Friendship, Less Business

In my opinion, Facebook and Twitter are the two social media biggies you should get involved with immediately. That said, I believe them to be completely different monsters. Whereas Twitter is an information-sharing site that you can use to educate yourself about news and the world, Facebook is a site geared toward sharing *personal* information, rather than professional updates. Both sites, however, definitely blend into gray concerning the personal/work boundaries.

I look at Facebook as something like a website/blog combo all about me personally. First and foremost, it's a means for me to stay in touch with family and friends as we all share updates and images from our lives. It's a remarkable way to connect with people who you would otherwise not hear from on a regular basis. It's up to you to decide who you want to allow to be your friend (outside of true family and friends). If you don't plan on befriending people you don't know personally, then Facebook ceases to become a platform tool—because you're purposefully limiting your reach—and you may want to skip this section.

I personally am very open to new friends on Facebook. I accept all friend requests unless a person gets heavy into religion, politics, or an inappropriate topic. Most of these people who befriend me have met me on Twitter, through my blog, or at an event. My Facebook is a chance for people to get beyond my work side and see me as a person—so I become relatable (Fundamental Principle #10).

Just as whom you befriend on the network is up to you and your approach, what exactly you post on Facebook is all up to you. While everyone will take a different approach, I can give you a quick start by showing you how I approach Facebook vs. Twitter. Examine these updates below and which site I'm more inclined to use:

> **UPDATE:** "New blog post about how to get short stories published—see it here and check out the book giveaway details (hyperlink)."
>
> **BEST FOR THE NETWORK(S) OF:** Twitter
>
> **REASON FOR MY CHOICE:** My blog is a business site all about educating yourself to get a literary agent. Business translates well to Twitter.

> **UPDATE:** "My dog has reached an epic level of laziness."
>
> **BEST FOR THE NETWORK(S) OF:** Facebook

REASON FOR MY CHOICE: This is personal and humorous—two characteristics that work better on Facebook. Plus, I would like to include a photo with this note. Facebook posts the photo right there on the page, whereas Twitter makes you click to another page to see an image.

UPDATE: "Very excited to announce my latest book deal!"
BEST FOR THE NETWORK(S) OF: Twitter and Facebook
REASON FOR MY CHOICE: This is big news in my professional/personal life, and big, exciting news like this does not come along often—so I don't feel guilty sharing it through all channels. When I tweet such news, I will include a link to a blog post about it, so people can learn more about the news. Facebook allows me space to properly explain the announcement. Other similar bits of good news I may promote through all channels would be a high-profile mention/review of my work or perhaps an upcoming class or conference session I'm teaching.

If you're unsure what to post in what social media networks (and that includes all kinds of niche networks we won't discuss in length), simply look at what others are doing—especially successful others—and take a cue from them. When in Rome ...

"My Facebook page is a fun way to keep in contact with family and friends, but it's also a great way to stay in touch with or even 'meet' my readers. For that reason, I'm careful about what I post. I try to post status updates, photos, and links that will not only be valuable to my readers, but will engage them in conversation. And when they leave comments, I'm sure to respond, because that's the benefit of social networking—that it provides a direct line to my readers without publishers, agents, or any other gatekeepers blocking my way."

—**PATRICIA V. DAVIS**, *author of* Harlot's Sauce *and* The Diva Doctrine

Successful Facebook Practices

- **MARKET SPARINGLY.** In my opinion, your self-marketing should only be about one-tenth of your total posts—and hopefully less. Facebook is a network for communicating with friends, so recognize that you must market only now and again.
- **MARKET BY NOT MARKETING.** Instead of saying, "Buy my book here," mention good news about your book to draw attention to it without using words like "buy" or "sell." If you get a really good review, say so. If someone interviewed you and the interview is online, mention it with a hyperlink (and include news of a giveaway if there is one). Share milestones, as well—like your one hundredth blog post. I recently saw a Facebook status update from a self-published woman who was celebrating the sale of her two thousandth book copy. Hey, it caught my attention...
- **TRY TO ENJOY YOURSELF.** Like blogging and Twitter, using Facebook will be a lot easier if you can find ways to enjoy yourself. You'll see that when you put salesmanship aside and simply try to start conversations about topics you enjoy, people will reach out to you more easily than you think.
- **MAKE FRIENDS AND HELP OTHERS.** Promote the works and causes of others. Share good news from friends and family. Start conversations on topics of interest (sports, pop culture, wondering who in the world still makes their bed in the morning).
- **CREATE A FAN PAGE.** When you start on Facebook, your default page will be a *profile page*—all about you. However, you can create fan pages about your book(s) or just about you as an author. Fan pages have no limit on how many people follow, and they serve as a business tool because people can follow instantly with one click (with no waiting for an "approval" from the creator). I'm not going to post news about my vacation on the fan page for *How*

to Survive a Garden Gnome Attack. Instead I'm going to post news about how we sold rights to Japan. A word of caution, though: If you start a fan page for a book, rather than yourself as an author, you run the risk of having several fan pages, diluting your support. Also, if you create a fan page and garner a lackluster number of fans, the page's existence will actually work against you when agents and editors put your platform under the microscope.

AND OTHER SOCIAL NETWORKS...

Again, I realize that this social networking section could encompass so much more, but space prohibits it. I just want to mention a few other big and interesting gathering places to have on your radar. Besides the few sites listed below, I urge you to do some basic research on anything that looks promising, be it Squidoo or StoryLink or something that's been invented since I wrote this paragraph.

- **GOODREADS.** Whereas big social networking sites like Facebook and Twitter are for all people, Goodreads (goodreads.com) is a site pretty much devoted to writers and readers. With the tagline "Meet your next favorite book," it's a site that gathers multitudes of book reviews, and lets you know what your friends are reading and have read. Beyond that, it sees what you've read and picks out similar books for future recommendations. Because Goodreads is a reader-heavy site and has promotion options for writers, I highly recommend making this one of your first social networking stops after you get on Facebook and Twitter.
- **GOOGLE +.** This is not your ordinary Google search engine. Google+ (https://plus.google.com) is a means to connect with those you know and round them into "circles"—clusters of friends based on your relationship to them, such as "sorority sisters," "co-workers," or "people who love fantasy football." At the time of writing this, Google+ has yet to go über-popular, but I think it soon will. In this social network, you tailor everything to different circles, but you're still pulling content from

one main hub. In other words, when you create content, you can allow everyone to see it (like a blog post), a select few to see it (like an e-mail to friends), or only one person to see it (almost like a letter). One downside is that it typically connects you with people you already know. If your goal is reach and platform, the whole point is to extend *outside* your current realm of influence.

- **LINKEDIN.** This site (LinkedIn.com) is primarily known for connecting individuals regarding business purposes—e.g., those looking to hire someone and those looking for a new/future job position. Though the site plays heavy into job hunting, it can benefit anybody. You can network with other professionals (remember: networking is crucial) and join groups of people that possess similar interests.

- **YOUTUBE.** This is a site (YouTube.com) people use to upload video content for free. From there, they can share the video easily on any website or blog they own. YouTube makes sharing video files effortless. Simply start an account, upload the videos (there are limits on video size and length), embed the videos online, and *voilà*. You can now vlog (video blog) and have readers see you as a person and not just some distant figure.

- **PINTEREST.** This fast-growing site (Pinterest.com) revolves around boards created for certain special interests—everything from crafts to botany to exercise. It's popular with women, and recipes seem to be a big part of the site so far. Your goal should be to create a board (or boards) that focus on subjects that you're interested in—or better yet, boards that relate to your brand and niche. For my humor titles, for example, I would create boards about gnome attacks as well as when dogs and politics combine.

- **FORUMS (VARIOUS).** A forum is simply a place where people can create threads about any topic and discuss anything. Forums are usually great places to meet like-minded writers and perhaps get your work critiqued by peers. If this interests you, start with the Writer's Digest Forum (writersdigest.com/forum).

CHAPTER 13

4 SIDE DOORS TO PLATFORM

If you can't climb over the mountain that is platform, are there ways that you can go around it, under it, or through it? Perhaps, but know that none of those ways are terribly easy, either. In this chapter, we will examine several possible avenues you can take that may help you cut corners in the world of author visibility.

But know this: Almost every nonfiction author I know has built his or her platform from the ground up. (The author case studies will back me up.) If you seek to be the exception and not the rule, you're adding daunting probability numbers to your journey. Furthermore, you're taking out the valuable element of career control that I discussed before. Lastly, even if you manage to get one book published by taking a unique roundabout route, what will you do when you want to sell Book #2?

Simply put, you need to be careful with shortcuts in the world of writing and platform. Think your decisions through. That said, I believe there are at least four varied and viable methods for going around typical roads and finding platform success. Perhaps one is of interest to you.

1. PAIR UP WITH A PLATFORM-HEAVY EXPERT AS YOUR CO-WRITER

Here's a situation I see often: a writer has a great book idea and solid credentials but no means to promote his or her own work. In this case, the writer is not lacking in all areas, but merely one—platform. So instead of constructing a platform from the ground up with a thousand small steps, pairing up with another individual can possibly accomplish all those tiny steps for you in one fell swoop.

If this platform-light writer described above sounds like you, your goal, should you choose this route, could be to look for an expert who is very much in the public eye—a contributor to TV shows, radio programs, and/or large publications. Look for someone who doesn't have any books to his or her name. Whether this is because the person doesn't enjoy writing or doesn't have the time is unimportant for now. What is important is that the individual is the opposite of you: He or she possesses a platform, but not the time/ability/drive to write a book. That's where you come in and complete a partnership.

Reach out to this other person when you have a solid book proposal drafted. Introduce the idea of writing a book together. Explain all about what the book is and why it's valuable—then get to the good news: *He or she will be doing little to no writing.* The expert's most valuable job in the partnership is to promote the heck out of the book, and it's up to both of you to come up with a dynamite marketing plan that exploits every opportunity at your (their) fingertips.

Obviously, explain that the more marketing that's done, the more money you will make. Also relay the benefit of how he or she will gain opportunities by being a published book author. (In other words, make sure you've practiced your pitch for the project. Your partner will need convincing.)

The reason this "partner" approach doesn't happen very often is because it has downsides. First of all, you'll be giving away a significant chunk of whatever money the book makes. Second of all, a serious clash of personalities is always a possibility. And the biggest challenge of all is finding someone who matches perfectly against your strengths and weaknesses so the collaboration works. Plus, your platform is diluted because the brand doesn't consist of your individual self.

2. TEAM UP WITH OTHER WRITERS AND START A GROUP

I see this "teamwork" approach happen a lot with novelists—especially writers who work in the same genre, such as the following:

- Minnesota Crime Wave (minnesotacrimewave.org): A trio of crime writers who live in Minnesota and base their works there.
- The Kill Zone (killzoneauthors.blogspot.com): Eleven successful thriller and mystery writers who blog on writing.
- The Liars Club (liarsclubphilly.com): A group of thirteen Philadelphia-area writers that work together to promote. The group has no particular genre focus, just a regional connection.

Earlier in the book I discussed the value both of having others guest blog for you and also of guest blogging for other people's larger sites. Guest blogging is beneficial to all parties involved and feeds directly into Fundamental Principle #2 of "You don't have to go it alone." The writers involved in this "teamwork" approach have taken this concept to the next level. When you have ten people in a group, you have ten people to provide blog content, not just one. You have ten people who promote the group's work through social media. You have ten different and unique mini platforms all helping each other sell books, all working for the greater good.

If you can find group members who work well together both in personality and where duties and workload are concerned, the teamwork approach can be an outstanding promotional boon for all involved. Marie Lamba is a member of The Liars Club and recently started taking on clients as a literary agent for Jennifer De Chiara Literary. "The Liars Club is proof that when it comes to building your writing career, there's strength in numbers," she says. "But we've noticed that there aren't many groups like ours out there; surprisingly few authors seem to have joined forces in a similar way."

Forming a small intense group should not be confused with joining a local chapter of a large organization. If you're a romance writer, for example, it's certainly wise to get involved with the Romance Writers of America (RWA) and seek out a local chapter to meet writing friends and find writing peers[1] for your work. But such a group can be quite large, and what you get out of your membership depends on what you put into it. A small group like The Kill Zone has a clear focus and purpose—with set duties and carefully chosen core members.

3. CONTRIBUTE TO AN EXISTING SERIES OF BOOKS

Sometimes it's not the author that garners visibility, but the *book series itself*. The biggest examples of this include the For Dummies series, The Everything Guide series, About.com, and The Complete Idiot's Guide series.

Let me ask you something: Have you ever bought one of these helpful guides because of who the writer was or what their brand was? Methinks not. You bought the book because you wanted a simple guide that could teach you about a subject or skill, and you trusted the name of the series. That means that a wise expert with a small-yet-growing platform could still have success writing an installment.

Before you think about pitching a new book in a series like this, make sure you're an unquestionable expert. If all you're bringing to the table is expertise, you better have it. "Credentials really do matter for the series," says Lisa Laing, managing editor of The Everything Guide series (Adams Media). "In the past, we used a lot of freelance writers— people who could write about anything or who had certain broad areas they wrote about (business, personal finance, parenting, health), but that's no longer true. 'Everything' writers must be experts in the field."

---

[1] Also called "beta readers."

Laing provided me with the three questions she asks when reviewing a prospective new "Everything" title:

1. What is the need for this book? Is there a growing trend? Are more people interested in the subject than in the past year or so? Does the subject have a growing buzz?
2. What would your book have that others on the subject don't have? What makes this book unique?
3. Why are you qualified to write this book?

So, do you need an excellent platform? Possibly not. Having a small platform may be acceptable. Literary agent Verna Dreisbach, who has sold many books to both The Complete Idiot's Guide and The Everything Guide series, says this: "Most times, [editors] want the writer to have already written at least one book so that they know that they can depend upon the writer to follow through and put out a good product."

4. HAVE BOATLOADS OF MEDIA CONTACTS

When I want to feature a writer in *Writer's Digest*, I start by Googling him or her. Most of the time, lots of websites and results turn up—but sometimes not so much. As I do a little research to learn more about these hard-to-find scribes, I usually find out that plenty are accomplished journalists, article writers of note, TV show staffers, or prolific short story authors. When you have success in the areas they've found success in (typically big-time journalism), you make a *lot* of key contacts in the media. You befriend book reviewers, news reporters, television producers, and others.

Which brings me to my point: These writers rely almost completely upon their contacts (friendship, favors, or both) and their constant article writing for their promotion and publicity. The fact is, incredible contacts or a long list of friends in the media can get agents' attention pretty fast and probably trump nuts-and-bolts platforms to a degree. "Journalists are like genre fiction authors—they tend to hang out together and support each other," says Hector DeJean, publicist for St. Martin's Press. "They have a rolodex full of contacts."

So if you have outstanding media contacts, know some movie stars on Twitter, or have relatives in the right places, your platform journey may be shorter than 99 percent of everyone else's … You lucky skunk.

THE VALUE OF CONTACTS AND NETWORKING

Have you ever signed a client who had a tremendous "old school" platform (plenty of newspaper contacts) but no "new school" platform (Twitter, blog, vlog)? If so, have editors voiced their concerns about lack of social media awareness even though the platform was good in other ways? (Or have you found the opposite—prejudice against those who have large Twitter followings but little else?)

> "This comes up primarily with young writers and seasoned academics. If the author is a recognized expert or the young writer seems like an up-and-comer, publishers will look past the lack of 'new school' platform. But it will be reflected in the advance."
> —**LAURIE ABKEMEIER** *(DeFiore and Company)*

> "I haven't seen any prejudice against 'new media' only, and I haven't seen any overt push back for authors who have only 'old school' platform. I think the major difference is that if they aren't using some sort of social media, it's a mentality that a) it doesn't work, b) it's only for young people and I'm too old for that, c) I don't like it, d) I will start it when I get a book deal—and I think that is where a problem can arise. If you don't want to connect with your audience and you are against using tools to do that, it tells me that you aren't interested in selling

books, and you don't fully understand the author's role in the current market."

—**ROSEANNE WELLS** (*Marianne Strong Literary Agency*)

"I think it all depends on the book. If it's a more academic nonfiction book premise—science/psychology/journalistic/history—then the bylines, if they're in prominent publications, are enough. If it's a more modern/trendy topic—pop culture/self-help/blog-to-book—then the platform typically has to be more in new media. This is intuitive, I think—wherever your audience is, that's where you need to be. Academic/serious nonfiction readers are still getting their recommendations from reviewers. The culture/self-help set is increasingly shifting to bloggers and social media for these recommendations."

—**MEREDITH BARNES** (*formerly of Lowenstein Associates, Inc.*)

"These days I think most authors do have some sense of what is going on in social media, but I still find some older authors who have not yet dipped a toe in the water. If I do find someone I want to work with who falls into the total newbie camp, I will try to get them started on this before putting anything in front of an editor. In the past year I've actually introduced two authors—one of whom founded a magazine some years ago, and the other who was a news correspondent for major papers some years ago—to blogging. It seemed weird to me that neither had been doing this from the time blogs existed, but both, needless to say, were very good once they began, and quickly found an audience that was interested in their perspectives. A word to the wise is sometimes all that's necessary to get this missing piece filled in. Conceptually, tweeting can be difficult for the old guard to grasp and not all of them will, but I usually will urge them to at least try—to take baby steps and see how they feel about it."

—**STEPHANY EVANS** (*FinePrint Literary Management*)

"With the conveniences (and inconveniences) of modern-day technology, it's important for clients with old school platforms to maintain those platforms but to conform and incorporate present-day practices of social networking. [Doing so] will allow the client to branch out and reach a more broad demographic."

—**SHAWNA MOREY** (*Folio Literary Management*)

"'Old school' is still a great way to get that contact with readers and build up a loyal fan base. Newspaper contacts can guarantee plenty of coverage, whether they're reviews, interviews, full features about your book, or just using you as a source when they do a story related to your topic. And plenty of public speaking gigs—*holy cow, where can I find you?* If you have a lot of one-on-one contact with potential buyers, or better yet, can arrange speaking engagements like seminars or workshops where the purchase of a copy of your book is included in the tuition to the class, publishers *love* that! I'm always certain in these cases, though, to make my case with numbers. *How many speaking engagements? How many attendees? Can you provide a list of the appearances from the previous six months and those already booked for six months to a year going forward?* Hard numbers are very convincing."

—**GINA PANETTIERI** (*Talcott Notch Literary Services*)

To further help writers understand how a platform comes to fruition, I reached out to twelve authors for lengthy interviews, which serve as case studies for platform creation. In this final section of the book, you will find the journeys of fiction authors, nonfiction authors, and memoir writers—all of whom found success by building their platforms from the ground up. They all took different roads and learned different things, and as a result, they all share different tips. Read what they have to say and learn from their roads to success.

AUTHOR CASE STUDIES

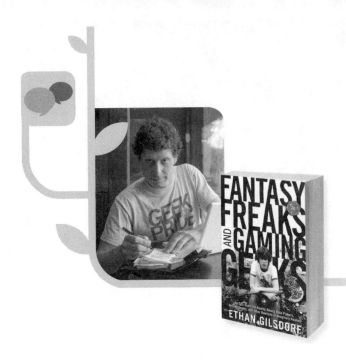

Ethan Gilsdorf

MEMOIR

Ethan Gilsdorf is the author of *Fantasy Freaks and Gaming Geeks: An Epic Quest for Reality Among Role Players, Online Gamers, and Other Dwellers of Imaginary Realms* (The Lyons Press, 2009), as well as a poet, teacher, critic, and journalist who has worked as a freelance correspondent, guidebook writer, and film, book, and restaurant reviewer. Based in Massachusetts, he publishes stories regularly in the *New York Times*, the *Boston Globe*, Salon.com, Wired.com, and the *Christian Science Monitor*, and has past credits in many other national publications. He is a book and film critic for the *Boston Globe*, film columnist for *Art New England*, and a core blogger for Wired.com's "Geek-Dad." Ethan's blog, "Geek Pride," is seen regularly on PsychologyToday.com. He also contributes to blogs at Boston.com's Globetrotting; Tor.com; and TheOneRing.net. Follow Ethan's fantasy adventures at fantasyfreaksbook.com.

When did you first start to stand out in your market?

My niche has now become fantasy, escapism, gaming, science fiction, movies, books, pop culture, and geek culture. I began by writing feature articles, reviews, and blog posts on these topics for such publications as the *Boston Globe*, the *New York Times*, the *Christian Science Monitor*, *Psychology Today*, and others. It was actually by realizing that I was writing in a focused way on these topics—it sort of snuck up on me that I was obsessed in some way with these topics—that I might be able to stand out in the marketplace. My growing interest in these topics, ranging from Harry Potter and *Lord of the Rings* fandom to epic literature to role-playing games like Dungeons & Dragons, led me to the idea that I might be able to write a book on the topic. I published more and more. The short pieces led me to the book. Having an expertise begat more opportunities to be an expert. At first, I felt a little like I wasn't sure what made me an expert. Eventually, as I wrote more and researched more about the niche topics that I loved, I realized I had something to offer. I feel strongly that I would not have caught the attention of my agent, the wonderful Sorche Fairbank, had I not already begun to establish myself as an expert in the media.

It also didn't hurt that I already had a network of dozens of publications that I wrote for. Not that I expected special treatment from them, but if you're a regular contributor to various print and web markets, you can expect that your book will at least be given an extra look. It doesn't hurt that if your shorter pieces appeared in, say, the *Washington Post*, and these shorter pieces later become a chapter in your book, that the *Post* might be interested in giving your book some coverage. At the very least, knowing the tech or education or arts editor at any given publication meant that when I was promoting a book tour event or trying to get coverage of my book, I had insiders who were willing to share names of their colleagues: the book review editor, for example, or the event-of-the-week picks editor.

A final word about that: Agents and editors want to be confident that a writer has connections to media and to opinion leaders in the field that the book is in. This is not only important for any media connections, but any connections to professional organizations, conventions, speaking engagements, universities, and radio or TV stations. Part of your platform building is also giving yourself the training and practice as a professional, well-spoken speaker. The more you can get that under your belt before you propose your book and try to get it sold, the better chance you have of getting a book deal.

Jumping forward to today, what do you consider the major aspects of your platform—the aspects that are largest and most helpful to selling books and making money?

Regarding blogging: Once I got some recognition in my field, I began to approach recognizable, name-brand sites (like Tor.com, Wired.com, etc.) to see if they would be interested in an occasional contribution from me. In some cases, this led to a regular blogging gig. I am still blogging on my own site—sometimes with links and pointers to these other blogs. The blogs give me a regular platform to be part of a conversation that feeds interest in my ongoing and future projects.

I still write a lot on these topics (fantasy, gaming, and geek culture), be it as a regular blogger to Wired.com or the *New York Times* or the *Boston Globe*. Every post or article (almost every one, anyway) ends with my bio, which mentions my book. That drives traffic to my website and to the various sites, such as Amazon, that sell my book. It's a little frustrating that I can't ever know for sure how my efforts are resulting in book sales; cause and effect is hard to map in the book business. But certainly after a popular post on Tor.com or Wired.com—or if someone mentions my book on some other site—I can see a spike in traffic to my site. Hopefully some of these lead to book sales.

The "making money" aspect has been the most surprising (and eye-opening). I'm not sure if my book will ever earn back its modest advance (and it's more than two years now since the hardcover came out and a year and a half since the paperback release). But I will say this: If I speak at a university, that's money in my pocket. An appearance at a convention may lead to a contact and later an invitation to blog for a high-profile publication or give a talk. An op-ed I write related to a topical issue that touches on my expertise is also a little money in my pocket. That same op-ed might be read by a talk show booker and lead to an appearance on a radio program. I also keep pitching myself to contacts I do have and try to tie in my appearances to timely topics that the show might be interested in. This also relates to the freelance feature stories I write. I can say, "I'm the author of *Fantasy Freaks and Gaming Geeks*" which gives me legitimacy to write more articles on the topic, even tangential topics. It's a self-perpetuating (sometimes vicious) cycle.

FYI: For every ten or fifteen pitches, I get one "yes." Sometimes it takes several pitches to finally get an assignment from an editor, an appearance on a radio show, or a speaking gig at a convention. You have to be patient, resilient, and consistent, and keep pitching.

So the moneymaking part of my career as an author is not made up of book sales alone. Having the book gives me a platform to keep talking about my areas of expertise, and many of these are paid gigs. So I try to see this more holistically and not get too grumpy about "Has my book made back its advance?" and "When will I get my royalties?" I've made thousands on speaking and writing, which are key revenue streams that, again, bolster your legitimacy as an expert and lead to more planks for your platform.

I do want to stress that having a book out there in print from an established publisher still opens doors and lends legitimacy, even in this world of online content, e-books, and self-publishing.

I'd also like to mention *networking* and paying people back for their kindnesses. If someone you know has a book to promote, help him or her. Post a blog about it or a Q&A with the author on your blog. If you're speaking at a convention, promote your event and the events of other authors and civilians. An essential part of your platform building is that you are also a fount of cool, new, interesting information in your field, and that means you can't only promote yourself and your events. Be generous, offer to help spread the word on cool stuff, and others will do the same for you.

What do you enjoy about platform building?

I feel I'm part of a larger conversation about the topics I love. Tweeting and posting on Facebook, Google+, and other social media can lead to new connections with people. It's great to see your posts retweeted and liked. (It's also easy to feel like that's all that matters.) And, of course, if you get someone to actually buy your book and they like it and write you to tell you how much they like it, then you feel like all your platform building is paying off. I also like networking—the feeling that I am part of a community of folks who are interested in the same topics.

What do you dislike about it?

Sometimes I feel like I'm putting a lot of myself out there, in little bits, spreading myself too thin, worrying about "likes" and page views. It's easy to get sucked into the superficial aspects of building a career as a writer and to become seduced by these shallower aspects. It's also distracting at times to be constantly blogging, promoting, and pitching—any of which can serve as a real impediment or a superficial excuse not to focus on the actual writing of the next book or engaging in the next project. Time spent on Twitter or Facebook is time you're not using to write your next book. I struggle with this constant-ly—the worry about where and how to best spend my time.

Look back at your road to writing success and try to identify the tipping points that influenced your platform.

I'm not sure I can comment on this since I don't think I've had any major tipping points in the way you are suggesting. But when I started getting offers for speaking gigs or guest blog positions, I guess you might say there was a tipping point. One quick example: I wrote a personal essay for a small on-line magazine that was later resold (via a syndication compa-ny I work with) to the big newspaper in Little Rock, Arkansas. A library director in Fayetteville, who is a big geek, read that story. She invited me to speak at her library, flew me down, and paid me an honorarium and all my expenses. So I'd say that was a good tipping point moment!

What opportunities have you had that have come through connections on social media?

I wouldn't say social media, per se, has directly led to oppor-tunities. Every now and again, someone "big" posts a link to a story I've written, or retweets it. Or people will track me down on Facebook. In the end, we communicate via e-mail or phone or Skype. I'm still a little frustrated by Twitter (partly because I don't spend a ton of time on it). And I don't have tons of fol-lowers (fewer than one thousand).

In your mind, what are you doing differently from others that leads to platform success?

I'm not sure that what I'm doing is different from anyone else. I do think I am realistic, relentless, and patient, and I expect to get about 5 percent return on all my efforts. I just keep trying all kinds of ideas and hope that some of them stick. I definitely focused a lot of my efforts in the first six months of my book's release, but I continue to push and put myself out there and still get occasional reviews or coverage of my book more than two and a half years after its publication.

What do you see as the future of your platform building?

More of the same. The hope is that as I get better known as a writer, I won't feel as compelled (and obsessed) to do all these things. The hope is that the books begin to sell themselves because I have already created a name for myself. But this may not happen. So I suspect and expect that for my next book, should I be so lucky to publish one, that I'll have to relaunch many of these efforts all over again.

Mignon Fogarty

NONFICTION—POPULAR REFERENCE

Mignon Fogarty is the creator of Grammar Girl and the founder and managing director of Quick and Dirty Tips. The Grammar Girl podcast has been downloaded more than 40 million times and has won many awards, including Best Education Podcast in the Podcast Awards (2007, 2008), iTunes Best Podcast (2007), and Best Classic Podcast (2008, 2009, 2010). Mignon has appeared as a guest on *The Oprah Winfrey Show*, and she has been featured in the *New York Times, BusinessWeek*, the *Washington Post*, CNN.com, and more. Her many books include *Grammar Girl's Quick and Dirty Tips for Better Writing* (*New York Times* bestseller), *101 Misused Words You'll Never Confuse Again* (*Washington Post* bestseller), and *Grammar Girl Presents the Ultimate Writing Guide for Students* (adopted by Scholastic). Mignon has a B.A. in English from the University of Washington in Seattle and an M.S. in biology from Stanford University. She lives in Nevada. Learn much more at www.grammar.quickanddirtytips.com.

When did you first start to stand out in your market?

I started the Grammar Girl podcast as a hobby without any intention of writing a book, but the podcast grew exponentially in the first six months and became a huge hit. I think the podcast succeeded because the timing was right—podcasts were new and growing—and the fun, friendly, helpful nature of Grammar Girl filled a niche that was missing. Most writing about grammar is snarky or condescending, and I truly wanted to help people.

Jumping forward to today, what do you consider the major aspects of your platform—the ones that are largest and most help you sell books and make money?

I have four large platforms, and I believe they are all important parts of my success:

- Podcast: approximately 700,000 downloads per month
- Twitter: more than 185,000 followers
- Facebook: more than 60,000 fans
- E-mail newsletter: more than 65,000 subscribers

All of these grow every month, so by the time this book comes out, they are likely to be much higher.

The podcast comes out every week, the e-mail newsletter comes out every week, and I post multiple times per day to Twitter and Facebook. I answer a lot of questions on Twitter and Facebook, too. I believe that delivering content on a regular schedule (the podcast and newsletter) helps people incorporate you into their media consumption ritual, and I believe that answering questions and interacting with followers is helpful (which reinforces my brand), makes people want to help me succeed, and helps people remember me when they are ready to buy a book.

What do you enjoy about platform building?

My platforms make it easy for people to tell me how my book or podcasts or newsletters have helped them, and I love to hear about that. I enjoy hearing people's questions because they give me ideas for future tips. I enjoy the peripheral effects of platform building, too, meeting people, interacting regularly with them, and occasionally becoming friends.

What do you dislike about it?

I hate getting the same question for the two thousandth time and having people ask me things they could easily (easily!) look up themselves. I hate people who demand an answer to their questions, but I also hate disappointing people when I can't answer their questions.

Look back at your road to writing success and try to identify the tipping points that influenced your platform.

Unfortunately, I have never been able to identify what propelled me to the top charts at iTunes, and that was the real tipping point for the podcast. It happened within the first six weeks, and once the podcast reached the top one hundred, it never fell out. Because I was a guest on *Oprah*, a lot of people think that must have been the tipping point, but it really wasn't. It gave my audiobook and print book a nice (but not stunning) boost in sales but didn't create much of a lasting traffic boost for the podcast or website. The publishing tipping point was clearly when the *Wall Street Journal* made my site their web pick of the day. Within a week, I was contacted by four major publishers and multiple agents.

What opportunities have you had that have come through connections on social media?

Especially early on, I got a ton of press coverage just from having a successful podcast. When it was just me producing my podcast by myself, my site was chosen as the *Wall Street Journal* web pick of the day, I was featured on CNN.com, in *BusinessWeek* and the *Arizona Republic*, and I was invited to be on *The Oprah Winfrey Show*. I've also gotten at least four or five speaking engagements from people who are Grammar Girl fans. Actually, it seems as if almost every opportunity I've gotten (aside from my books) originated from a fan.

In your mind, what are you doing differently from others that leads to platform success?

It was not my plan to do this! I was a busy, successful technical writer when Grammar Girl hit, and I continued that work for about six months. When I got the first book contract, I was able to quit freelancing and devote myself to Grammar Girl full time. I work very, very hard on my platforms. I probably spend at least twenty hours per week on Twitter and Facebook, and I used to personally answer at least fifty questions a week by e-mail (I now have an assistant who does that for me since so many of the questions are repetitive). It's not easy to put out a well-researched podcast every week. Maintaining the Grammar Girl platform and writing Grammar Girl books is an intense, full-time job. I've been doing it nonstop for almost six years and for the most part, the growth has been steady rather than in bursts.

To be clear, when I say to post to Twitter and Facebook multiple times each day, that includes links to other people's work. I do post links to everything I create myself, but I also post links to interesting language articles that other people have written. I do it because I find things interesting and feel compelled to share, but the experts would say that by doing so, I turn myself into a trusted expert instead of someone who people perceive as focused on promoting her own work. I didn't start doing it with such calculated motives, but in retrospect, I can see that it's part of what made me successful on social media.

How do you translate your visibility in the marketplace into making money?

I make money from the advertising in my podcasts and from book sales. I don't enjoy speaking, but I do four to six engagements a year just because it's nice supplemental income and I have a hard time saying no. I could do much more speaking if I wanted to. I always enjoy meeting the people at my talks; I just don't like the travel and preparation.

If you could go back in time and do it all over again, what would you tell your younger self in terms of platform?

I knocked myself out for a year doing my e-mail newsletter every day and for one quarter doing my podcast twice a week—and in retrospect, I don't think it was worth the effort. Weekly is enough. The benefit from publishing daily and podcasting twice a week was minimal.

What do you see as the future of your platform building?

Just to keep up! I'm only half kidding. I'd like to build a video platform, but that's been on my to-do list for a couple of years. I keep an eye on new social media networks, and jump in when they seem to be getting traction. I recently started using Pinterest and Google+ for example, and they seem like ones I might stay with.

Is there anything else you would like to add?

I think you really have to *enjoy* interacting on social networks or you won't do it well or stay with it. You can't force yourself to do it; you have to find the things you like and do those even if they aren't the most popular. For one person it might be Twitter, for another LinkedIn, for another YouTube, for another podcasting, and another blogging.

Also, I think some authors are too afraid to ask people to buy their book. I spend hours (and hours and hours) of my time answering people's questions without compensation, so when I have a new book out, I don't hesitate to post about it. I believe I've earned the right to marketing my products. On the other extreme, I see a lot of authors jump into Twitter and immediately start doing nothing but push their book. They haven't earned the right to market their products, and all they do is turn people off.

Mary Kole

NONFICTION—WRITING REFERENCE

Mary Kole is a literary agent and author. She is the author of the book *Writing Irresistible Kidlit: The Ultimate Guide to Crafting Fiction for Young Adult and Middle Grade Readers* (Writer's Digest Books, 2012). A senior literary manager with Movable Type Management (formerly with the Andrea Brown Literary Agency), she represents children's book authors and illustrators, and is a frequent speaker at writers conferences nationally and internationally. Some of the books she's represented include *Through to You* by Emily Hainsworth (young adult, 2012), *Wildfire* by Karston Knight (young adult, 2011), and *When Blue Met Egg* by Lindsay Ward (picture book, 2012). Mary's writing-related blog, Kidlit.com, is an ongoing project for the passionate community of people who read and write children's literature and has been named to the Writer's Digest "101 Best Websites for Writers" list multiple times.

When did you first start to stand out in your market?

Growing up in the Silicon Valley, I have always had a compulsion to be out there on the Internet. My first website was *The X-Files* fan fiction choose-your-own-adventure game that I wrote and coded on GeoCities when I was twelve, back when people were just transitioning away from AOL and to the Internet at large. (Why, yes, I know exactly what you're thinking … I was very popular in middle school.) I did several blogs, each one short-lived but with lessons to teach. I also worked for several websites in the dot-com world.

When I knew I'd be joining [my first agency] the Andrea Brown Literary Agency as an agent, I decided to brand myself as a children's book expert, teacher, and blogger. Someone was squatting on the kidlit.com domain and I vividly remember deciding to buy it. I had to have that word, that term, that concept. The sales rep from my web hosting company called to report the domain owner's asking price. I stood there, my heart pounding, and okayed the purchase for what was an outlandish amount of money for me at the time. But I knew I wanted to brand myself. My goal for the blog initially was to get my name out there and make a splash with agenting right out of the gate. I also wanted to do it in a public way because my secondary goal was to attract writers and submissions specifically to *me*. I have eight amazing and more established colleagues, and I wanted to stand out. That's not all there is to it, of course—I love reaching out to writers, writing about writing, and teaching. But the blog was strategic from the get-go and, while a book deal for myself wasn't my initial goal, it's just one of the many ways in which platform changed my life.

Jumping forward to today, what do you consider the major aspects of your platform—the ones that are largest and most help you sell books and make money?

My platform is actually pretty typical—even lazy. I have three blogs: Kidlit.com, which I update twice a week; ChowLit.com, which is a hobby blog that gets maybe two posts a month; and KidlitApps.com, which is on about the same schedule. I also have a Facebook profile (not even a Facebook fan page), a Twitter feed, and an opt-in e-mail newsletter that I blast to subscribers with no specific regularity or promise of exclusive content. It's basically Social Networking 101.

In terms of my audience, I'm in the catbird seat, really, because I'm an agent. I'm in a perceived position of power. My audience flocks to me because I potentially hold the keys to making their dreams come true. So they follow me on Twitter, they comment on the blog, and they are all very lovely and nice. It's been embarrassingly easy, therefore, to build up my numbers and following. But herein lies the main secret, at least in my mind, of the Internet: People are self-centered (meant in the best way possible) and use the Internet to get what they want. We use the Internet with purpose always—even if that purpose is "I want mindless procrastination." You go online to figure out how to get that stain out of your carpet or how to cook a delicious braised lamb. If you have what your audience wants, they will flock to you. In my case, my audience wants me as an agent, or they want information about agents in general, or they want children's book publishing or writing tips. And here is where I use the main secret of the Internet to my advantage: I work very hard to write good content that serves the needs of my audience. It begins and ends there. My blog is not about me, it's about what my reader needs, and that, above all, is what draws them to me. The other stuff helps me market to them when I need to, but it wouldn't be there if it wasn't for my blog providing strong content.

What do you enjoy about platform building?

The blogging, hands down. The blog is a constant challenge and inspiration for me. I'm passionate about my subject— and because my readers are terrific. It also doesn't hurt that I love the sound of my own voice and enjoy broadcasting my opinions!

What do you dislike about it?

The social networking. As I mentioned, I'm lazy at it. I don't really engage on Facebook or Twitter as much as most because I don't really have to. My audience is eager and built-in. I don't reciprocate, comment, "like," retweet, nearly as much as most others who are actively building platform—because that's a rabbit hole I don't want to go down. There are only so many hours in a day. Ideally, good social networking is a two-way street, an exchange between you and your readers. In that same vein, I hate it when there's a lot of stuff I need to market to my audience—upcoming conferences or whatever—because then I really feel like a bullhorn blaring at them. I never want to alienate my audience by making the transparent sales message the *only* message.

Look back at your road to writing success and try to identify the tipping points that influenced your platform.

I can't remember any one tipping point in particular, but my bumps in traffic and attention have all come from the generosity of other writing teachers like Nathan Bransford, Cynthia Leitich Smith, Debbie Ridpath Ohi, and others. They were among the first to mention my articles, share, retweet. I am always surprised when people I admire recommend my blog posts, and I'm always grateful. The biggest synergy for me to date has been partnering with Writer's Digest because we share the same audience: people who have writing and publishing dreams.

What opportunities have you had that have come through connections on social media?

My blog has accomplished a lot for me, both exactly what I set out to do with it and more unexpected things. Because of the strength of my content (and I'm not being egotistical—this is my number one goal and something I work hard to accomplish), I have gotten the exact reputation I wanted: expert. This has opened many doors, including my book, the opportunity to teach webinars, conference speaking invitations, and other things. There have also been unexpected benefits: I now have blog friends, some of whom I'm very close to. I also had a blog reader write to me and ask me when I was coming to Japan. So I referred him to his local branch of the SCBWI, a children's writing organization that tours me around quite a bit, and they ended up flying me out to both Japan and Hong Kong to speak. That never would've happened if a blog reader hadn't found me and requested me! Another great thing I did as a result of my blog following was raise over $10,000 in an online auction for Tennessee flood relief by donating manuscript critiques. I cried when I found out the grand total of my efforts. People found me and connected with me over the blog (which is basically just me being myself and talking about what I love) and, as a result, we were able to make an actual difference in the world.

In your mind, what are you doing differently from others that leads to platform success?

My unique position as an agent, as I've said, has a lot to do with it. But my core principles have never wavered: good content that's useful to the reader. Still, I feel like it's early days for my platform and that I could always be better at it. I don't know if that's a useless resolution, but the Internet and social media are constantly evolving, so I'm sure I will keep evolving my platform skill set right along with it. Having a book to sell soon will teach me a lot, I think.

How do you translate your visibility in the marketplace into making money?

My biggest moneymakers so far are writers conferences and the webinars I teach for Writer's Digest. The former is twofold: The blog helps attract conference organizers who invite me to events *and* it reaches potential conference attendees. Not only can I demonstrate that I'll have lots to say at a conference, but I am also an asset because I can promote the show and drive sign-ups ("You love the blog, now come meet me in person in Utah!"). The webinars are very interesting because they are a concrete measure of my platform muscle. When I blog or tweet about a webinar, I use a reference code in the link and then I can actually see how many clicks and, more important, how many conversions (purchases) my social media outreach efforts have yielded. The number of sign-ups translates directly into what my paycheck will be. The webinars have been going really well so far, but it's also intimidating. The webinars are my platform completely exposed: Every time I see the attendee total, I know that that's what my social networking "net worth" is at that given moment.

If you could go back in time and do it all over again, what would you tell your younger self in terms of platform?

This may sound like bad advice but: Blog less! I was killing myself trying to blog three times a week at Kidlit, then I added two extra blogs and tried doing those twice a week, too. The result? I'd travel or freak out and let the blogs go to seed for a while, and that was altogether worse than blogging less frequently because dead blogs and silence are the ultimate online networking sins. It's very possible to have a platform with the "less is more" philosophy, as long as you focus on the absolute quality of your efforts.

What do you see as the future of your platform building?

I do believe in the "long-tail" philosophy and think that platforms will get more specific in the future. Right now, the buzzword is *curating*. Everyone is a curator of something and they all do it over on Tumblr. But I don't know if a platform of a curator randomly telling people about random cool stuff has legs, or if it can easily be monetized. If you don't already have one, find a strong niche and drill deeply into it. That's the other thing I can account for my success: I picked a field, I branded myself from day one, and I have found or created enough to discuss within that field that I'm good for years.

Is there anything else you would like to add?

I have gotten flack for saying this before, but I am sticking to my guns: Do it well or don't do it at all. There are billions of websites out there. On the Internet, if you build it, they will *not* automatically come. You have to give people a good reason to spend their precious time on *your* real estate. Don't blog or tweet or Facebook because you think you have to. Your reluctance will ooze from the screen. Don't engage if you can't keep it consistent, both in terms of timing and in terms of quality. Figure out what you're best at, then do that well and forget the other stuff. You should have *some* online presence, but you don't have to jump into everything all at once, especially if you're going to do it badly or irregularly. And especially in terms of publishing, if you're a writer, remember that your strongest piece of marketing lies between the covers of your book. Nobody's going to invest dollars and reading hours in your career because of your awesome Flickr photostream. Nobody's going to recommend your book to friends because of your hilarious Facebook cat pictures. Get the online component of your platform sorted out, keep up with it at your own pace, and then write the best books you can because that's what matters at the end of the day.

Gina Holmes

FICTION—INSPIRATIONAL

Gina Holmes is the founder of Inspireafire.com and NovelRocket.com. She is the award-winning author of the faith-based novels *Crossing Oceans* and *Dry as Rain*. In 1998, Gina began her career penning articles and short stories. She holds degrees in science and nursing, and currently resides with her husband and children in southern Virginia. She works too hard, laughs too loud, and longs to see others heal from their past and discover their God-given purpose. To learn more, visit ginaholmes.com.

When did you first start to stand out in your market?

> I started by launching a blog called Novel Journey. The name has changed a few times and has now settled into Novel-Rocket.com, but the mission has only changed once. I originally began it on the advice of a friend, who said that every writer ought to have a blog to build a platform. I didn't have

much idea back then what a platform was, but I trusted that he knew more than I did. Originally the blog chronicled my road to publication, but after many months and rejection letters, I was wondering just how interesting this really was to others, so I added a site meter. To my chagrin, I learned that we had three readers and one of them was me!

I was ready to fold up shop when one day I realized that I spent a lot of time on Google searching for the few-and-far-between author interviews that would tell me how authors before me had become successful. Then it hit me: If I was interested in this, then others probably were, too. My focus then changed from building a platform to helping other authors promote their novels as I worked and waited for my big shot.

That was back in 2004 before the gazillion author interview websites sprang up. I posted my first author interview and our hits skyrocketed. After a year or so, the site was getting to be too much for just me, so I brought on two of my critique partners, Ane Mulligan and Jessica Dotta, to share the work and platform. We've since enjoyed being one of the most well-read and revered site of our kind in the industry, have been named regularly as one of Writers Digest's best websites for writers, and are read by tens of thousands each month. And to think, I was one click away from deleting it all!

I think we've been so successful for several reasons. One is we fill a need. The second is we don't make it all about us. We don't just post what we would like to write or read, but what we think our readership would be interested in. The third reason I think we've been successful is that we take what we do very seriously. We treat it as a job and when someone tries to post something halfhearted, we call them on it. We expect excellence, and get it, from each team member and guest blogger. We try our best to make sure there are no "broken windows," as referenced in *The Tipping Point*. Meaning, if a link is broken, we fix it, if someone brings a typo to our notice, we fix it and so forth. We also interact heavily with our readers so they feel they know us personally. And they do.

Jumping forward to today, what do you consider the major aspects of your platform—the ones that are largest and most help you sell books and make money?

I was blessed enough to hit the bestseller list with my debut novel, *Crossing Oceans*. I think a big part of that was the platform I'd built with Novel Rocket. Of course, the book had to hold its own and it earned a lot of word-of-mouth sales, but would it have if I hadn't had the platform of the website to let people know about it? I'm not so sure. Novel Rocket and our slow build of readership was the push that sent the snowball down the hill and eventually caused an avalanche. Now with the success of my novels, I'm not sure if my bigger platform is the writing itself or the website.

What do you enjoy about platform building?

I totally *get* the marketing side of things—what works, what doesn't. I could have just as easily been in public relations as novel writing. I enjoy the psychology of PR, and building a platform has everything to do with that. I enjoy building a platform that others who aren't quite as technically minded as I am (and honestly, that ain't much!) can stand on as well. I enjoy the puzzle of it.

What do you dislike about it?

Like most writers, I would rather be writing than anything else. Each day, I take hours for PR, which in turn builds my platform brick by tedious brick. Some days, like today, I'd rather be writing a new chapter or editing an old one, but I take the time to fix my website, answer reader e-mails, do a couple of interviews to the best of my ability. This is all so time-consuming, but also necessary and a blessing even if it doesn't always feel like one. Some day, I hope, my platform will be built and sturdy, and I won't have to say yes to most everything as I do now. But until that happens, I build, slowly and surely.

Look back at your road to writing success and try to identify the tipping points that influenced your platform.

Jane Friedman picking up my post, "The 10 Things You Can Do Now to Promote the Novel You Haven't Even Sold Yet," and sending it out all over the Twitter universe certainly gave us a boost, as have interviews with some of the best-known authors. But for us, even with these pushes, it has ultimately been a slow build.

What opportunities have you had that have come through connections on social media?

I've definitely sold a lot of books just though mentions by myself—and more so through word-of-mouth mentions from other Facebook friends. Social media seems to get the most tangible and immediate sales. Someone can post that my book moved them to tears and next thing I know my Amazon rank has shot up. I've also made a lot of industry and reader friends, which have resulted in speaking engagements with conferences and book clubs, which in turn lead to more sales.

In your mind, what are you doing differently from others that leads to platform success?

What I see over and over again are writers who want to be published but don't want to write ... who want to sell books but don't want to promote ... who want to get a big book contract but don't want to endure all the rejection that comes before that big break. Recently I sat on a panel of writers, editors, and agents who were discussing ways how writers who are shy can promote their books. The funny thing is: I'm an introvert. It's uncomfortable to put myself out there—to stand in front of hundreds of other writers and talk about what I'm doing to forge my path in this overcrowded world of books—but I do it. It takes time away from writing and family, and the things I'd rather be doing, but I do it. And what I see the most successful writers doing is everything they touch [is done] to the best of their abilities. If they're asked for an interview, they put thought and time into it. Not all writers do that. Many throw down a first draft and call it a book. Throw down a sound byte or two and call it an interview. Get two rejection letters and call themselves a failure. Yes, it's all very difficult and time-consuming, but that's what success calls for. If it were easy, everyone would be doing it. Folks who are building a platform and name for themselves are not members in some secret club. They're just hard workers who understand that anything worth having is worth working their butt off for.

How do you translate your visibility in the marketplace into making money?

I honestly don't think that *Crossing Oceans* would have been as widely read as it is if I hadn't spent years building a platform beforehand. This base of readers had been watching and reading about my road to publication for years, and they were rooting for me. Having a large platform before I got the contract helped get me a far bigger advance than another author with the same book would have gotten. It also helps not just myself but other authors and team members get the word out about their books. In recent years, we've accepted advertisements, which helps defer the costs of running the site. I've also gotten speaking gigs that help pay the bills, so all in all, starting the site turned out to be worth all the hard work.

If you could go back in time and do it all over again, what would you tell your younger self in terms of platform?

I would tell myself that helping others succeed would translate into the biggest personal success. I would tell myself to go ahead and build my wings on the way down, and not to stress over every little number, setback, or failure.

Cal Newport

NONFICTION—EDUCATION

Cal Newport is an assistant professor of computer science at Georgetown University. He previously earned his Ph.D. in electrical engineering and computer science from MIT in 2009, and graduated Phi Beta Kappa from Dartmouth College in 2004. Newport is the author of three books of unconventional advice for students, which have sold a combined total of more than 100,000 copies: *How to Be a High School Superstar* (Random House, 2010), *How to Become a Straight-A Student* (Random House, 2006), and *How to Win at College* (Random House, 2005). His fourth book, a contrarian look at career advice, will be published by Grand Central in September 2012. In his role as a student success expert, Newport has appeared on ABC, NBC, and CBS and on over fifty radio networks. His Study Hacks blog (calnewport.com/blog), which offers advice to both students and graduates, attracts more than 100,000 unique visitors a month.

When did you first start to stand out in your market?

I published my first two books before I had any significant author platform beyond a simple website. Their sales were solid based on table placement in bookstores, strong titles, and good word of mouth.

Soon after the publication of my second book, I started an e-mail newsletter as a way to keep the conversation alive with my readers. After forty or fifty readers signed up, I realized that a blog made more sense—as it would make the information we were discussing public and reachable by a wider audience. It was the summer of 2007 when I started the blog. I called it Study Hacks. It took a few months to build up to a triple digit number of RSS/e-mail subscribers. Today that numbers stands around 25,000. In addition to the subscribers, in the last full month before answering these questions, I had 123,608 unique visitors to the site.

The rough timeline of the blog's growth proceeds as follows:

I started by writing about advanced studying, paper writing, and time management tactics for students. This was the same material covered in my first two books. In some sense, my blog, at this point, served as a source of extra material. If you liked the books and wanted more, you'd be pleased with what you found at Study Hacks. Call this Stage 1. During Stage 1, the blog has a clear philosophy: Advanced tactics can lead to a much more successful student experience.

One of the benefits of the blog is that it put me in touch, through e-mail, with my readers. I made a policy of trying to answer any questions that readers sent me via e-mail (which, today, translates to roughly one thousand questions answered per year). This helped me hone in on the issues that really mattered to my audience. After a year or two of this communication, I picked up that stress was a significant problem among American students. Their quest to be successful was leading to burnout, and there really was no useful advice out there for them outside of a binary choice between either sucking it up or lowering their ambition.

This realization led my blog to Stage 2. During Stage 2, my content began to shift away from tactics and shift toward describing and promoting a new model of student success, which I called the Zen Valedictorian. I made the claim that it is possible to be both relaxed and highly successful as a student. Then I set out to systematically validate this philosophy through case study after case study, and numerous tactical articles. This philosophy resonated at a deeper level than the Stage 1 philosophy, and my readership grew more. Subscribers moved past one thousand, then past five thousand.

Around this point, I sold my third book. It explored my Zen Valedictorian philosophy in the specific context of college admissions, showing students how it was possible to do well in college admissions while still enjoying high school life. The growing size of my platform certainly helped make this sale. More important, however, it was the interaction with readers and their feedback to my evolving writing that led to the ideas the book was based on. If I hadn't been writing Study Hacks for the two years leading up to my third book, the book never would have existed.

Around a year ago, the blog shifted into Stage 3, where I began to look at life after graduation, and I started asking, with my now-known contrarian, highly tactical perspective, how people end up with remarkable lives. Given the larger size of this audience, my readership really took off at this point, pushing me to my current numbers.

The back and forth I shared with my audience helped me develop and validate a sophisticated philosophy on how people end up loving what they do. At it's core was a rejection of the simplistic advice: Follow your passion. Last spring, I sold my fourth book, which explained this philosophy. It was sold at auction and is my first hardcover. It's titled *So Good They Can't*

Ignore You: Why Skills Trump Passion in the Quest for Work You Love. It came out in September 2012.

Jumping forward to today, what do you consider the major aspects of your platform—the ones that are largest and most help you sell books and make money?

My platform consists only of my blog and the open e-mail address I give for my readers to ask questions about the content. I have never had a Facebook account. I have never had a Twitter account. I don't know what Google+ means. I don't use them because I'm a professor, and I'm busy, and I find them too distracting. Their absence has not stopped my platform from being very valuable. I think this is an important point. What made my platform valuable is that it offered valuable information that tied into a clear philosophy that resonated with readers. In other words, I treated my blog like a book proposal: The onus was on me to convince the world that it *had* to read what I had to say.

What do you enjoy about platform building?

Developing content that resonates deeply with someone. It's a compelling challenge that never gets old.

What do you dislike about it?

I've eliminated the tedious. What matters is the content. I write good content as often as I can. That's my only obligation to my platform.

What opportunities have you had that have come through connections on social media?

Once a blog gets to a certain size, your content begins to spread widely. For me, this has certainly helped reporters find me when researching articles. It has also lead to the opportunity to meet many interesting people—many of whom have ended up as important interview subjects in my books.

In your mind, what are you doing differently from others that

leads to platform success?

> My obsessive focus on the reader has differentiated me some. I feel like every blog post is a book proposal: It is on me to [draw] people's attention. I think a lot of writing on platform success focuses too much on the technical optimizations, like connecting things to Twitter; or noncontent related strategies, like trying to do guest posts and using multimedia—that take attention away from the core of presenting ideas that resonate deeply with people.

How do you translate your visibility in the marketplace into making money?

> Right now the visibility helps me sell books. I mean this in several ways. Having a platform helps convince a publisher to invest in you. It also helps you sell copies once a book is published. Of equal importance to me, however, is that the platform is an idea laboratory, allowing me to sift through ideas and polish them to a devastatingly compelling sheen before bringing them to the world of print publishing.

What do you see as the future of your platform building?

> At this point, two topics are of great interest to me related to my platform. First, I am interested in more sophisticated ways of organizing the material I produce online. A chronological list of posts with category tags is okay, but there are probably more direct ways to connect a user who has a specific deep interest to exactly the right material. Second, I am interested in introducing some sort of nonfree service. More and more people are recognizing that the nonfiction author of the future will have a steady income from his or her platform, with print books being an occasional injection of extra income. How, exactly, this model will work is being sorted out right now, but I feel like I should be a part of that effort.

Lissa Rankin, M.D.

NONFICTION—HEALTH

Lissa Rankin, M.D., is an integrative medicine physician, author, speaker, artist, and founder of the online health and wellness community OwningPink.com. Dr. Rankin has been featured on over thirty television shows, on over fifty radio shows including *Oprah Radio*, as well as publications such as the *New York Times*, *Health*, *Women's Health*, *Forbes*, and *Woman's Day*, among many others. She is now leading a "Pink Medicine Revolution" to help patients heal themselves, while aiming to feminize how health care is received and delivered by encouraging collaboration, reconnecting health care and spirituality, and empowering patients to tap into the mind's power to heal the body. She will be sharing her scientific findings in her upcoming book *Mind Over Medicine: Scientific Proof You Can Heal Yourself* (Hay House, 2013). Her published books include the health book *What's Up Down There? Questions You'd Only Ask Your Gynecologist If She Was*

Your Best Friend (St. Martin's Griffin, 2010) and the art book *Encaustic Art: The Complete Guide to Creating Fine Art With Wax* (Watson-Guptill, 2010).

When did you first start to stand out in your market?

In 2007, I spent a year writing a memoir that a literary agent adored and eight editors wanted to publish. But eight marketing departments said, "We've never heard of her." After thirty-some rejections, my agent and I had a tearful release ceremony, as I burned manuscript pages and let the book go.

Afterwards, my agent said, "Honey, you need to start a blog." And so, in April of 2009, I started a little blog I called OwningPink.com, the story of how I had lost my mojo and how I would get it back. In order to attract readers, I started a Twitter profile, joined Facebook, and started posting *a lot* in a style similar to the writing style of my book (very vulnerable, authentic, and "girlfriendy"). Within three months, I had 100,000 readers, thirty thousand Twitter followers, thirty guest bloggers posting on my site about how they got their mojo back and how they've learned to help others heal, five hundred members in a Ning.com forum I started, and a mention in *Forbes* as one of the "20 Inspiring Women to Follow on Twitter."

Why did I succeed? When I decided to put my story out there in the world, I committed to being what I called "unapologetically *me*." I wasn't going to hide behind my M.D. title. I had a strict "un-guru" policy, and I let people in behind the white coat. I am a doctor, but I am also a professional artist, a mom, a daughter, a wife, a writer, and a perfectly imperfect human being, along with all the foibles that go along with being a spirit living in a body. I exposed stuff on my blog and on social media people almost never talk about (my publishing failure, my mommy issues, my sex life, the traumas of my medical education, my business *faux pas*), and people saw in me parts of themselves.

I led by example, and people started following me like they were watching a soap opera. They weren't sure whether I was an inspired visionary or a cautionary tale. Then three months after I started my blog and exploded my platform, I got two book deals in a month. My mantra at the time was "I'm on the right path, even if I don't know where I'm going." But I invited my readers to come along for the ride, and we're still navigating this journey of life together.

Jumping forward to today, what do you consider the major aspects of your platform—the ones that are largest and most helpful for selling books and making money?

My newsletter list is the most effective sales tool I have. Because these people have opted in and allowed me into their in-box, they are the most receptive audience, eager to read more of what I write and support me on my journey.

My blog at OwningPink.com is my group of core readers but I also syndicate my blog at Care2.com, PsychologyToday.com, and BlogHer.com, which helps me reach more people with the content I write three times a week.

Twitter has been almost magical as a tool for networking, reaching new people, and expanding my audience. In my opinion, Twitter is the law of attraction in action. If you put yourself out there in an authentic way, your tribe will find you. Via Twitter, I met almost all the bloggers who write for OwningPink.com. I met Dr. Christiane Northrup, who wrote the foreword to *What's Up Down There?*, and I've connected with almost all the celebrity doctors and healers I interviewed for *Mind Over Medicine*.

In addition to many celebrity authors who have become personal friends, my platform also includes an extensive network of media contacts (magazine editors, TV producers, radio show hosts, and others) who are interested in my work because they've worked with me in the past and are excited to support me when I write new books.

What do you enjoy about platform building?

The people. I have met some of the most incredible, high-vibration, open-hearted, inspiring, service-oriented, visionary human beings on the planet. My little blog also served as a massive healing force for myself, and once I got done licking my wounds, my platform put me in touch with my true calling—to revolutionize how health care is delivered and received, and to open us all to the healing power of the mind, heart, and spirit.

What do you dislike about it?

I spend way too much time at my Mac and on my telephone! I crave live human contact these days and am busy creating new ways to interact with my platform on stage, in workshops, in conferences, and in other live venues where I can actually hug people.

Look back at your road to writing success and try to identify the tipping points that influenced your platform.

The first tipping point came the day I launched OwningPink. com. A few days before I was supposed to launch, Twitter was all *atwitter* with the inflammatory, scary, incorrect information about swine flu. The graphic design of my site wasn't even done, but I decided to launch early, and the first post I put up was "17 Ways to Avoid Swine Flu and Why Not to Freak Out." I was on Twitter all day long, answering questions, trying to calm people down, being a voice of reason, and guiding them to my new blog. My first post got over ten thousand hits in a day. Once things calmed down about swine flu, I started blogging about what I wanted to blog about—how to heal yourself.

The next tipping point came when *Forbes* named me among the twenty inspiring women to follow on Twitter, and shortly afterwards, The Huffington Post named me among the "16 Health Experts to Check Out on Twitter." I doubled my Twitter following almost overnight.

The next big tipping point came recently. I delivered a TEDx talk in December 2011 called "The Shocking Truth About Your Health." People resonated so deeply with this talk (it starts out by saying, "What if I told you caring for your body was the *least* important part of your health?") that it got fifty thousand hits in its first forty-five days, putting it among the top 1 percent of all twelve thousand–plus TEDx videos ever posted on YouTube. My blog traffic has tripled since then, and my social media following has grown significantly with exactly the people I want in my network—those who are interested in self-healing and are committed to helping me serve out my mission, to heal our broken health care system and reclaim the heart of medicine.

What opportunities have you had that have come through connections on social media?

I had a fantasy that Dr. Christiane Northrup, my longtime hero, would write the foreword to *What's Up Down There?* So I tweeted my desire, and one of my followers tweeted back, "She's my best friend's mother. Let me introduce you." The rest is history!

When my second book came out, I hired a publicist, but almost every publicity opportunity came directly to me via Twitter and Facebook, including articles in *Glamour*, *Cosmopolitan*, the *New York Times*, WebMD, AOL, Fox News, *Woman's Day*, CNN, AOL, *Forbes*, The Huffington Post, and several local TV programs. I've done very little to actively pursue media opportunities, yet now I get so many, I'm turning some away because I just can't keep up. Now I'm blessed to be able to be very selective, screening media opportunities to keep myself available for the great ones that really help me spread my message.

In your mind, what are you doing differently from others that leads to platform success?

Very few doctors are allowing themselves to be so human on the Internet. Plus, I'm not just blogging and tweeting and posting in order to build my platform. I'm doing it because I love people. I'm called to be a healer, I'm devoted to my message, I'm passionate about fulfilling my life purpose, I'm committed to being unapologetically me, and I think people find it refreshing. Also, I'm a damn good writer. I consider myself a writer before a doctor, so spreading a message in writing on the Internet is so natural for me. I love it. It goes to the core of who I am, and I think people can see that. What you see is what you get. I think people can tell the difference, and they're naturally attracted to those who are shining their light in a genuine way, guided not by the desire to sell books, but the desire to serve.

For me, Twitter has been less effective at translating into book sales. I suspect that, because so many people tweet from their phones, they are less likely to click through to a sales page link in order to order the book. However, it has been wonderful at helping me meet people with big newsletter lists who send out solo blasts on my behalf in order to help me sell my books and online programs.

How do you translate your visibility in the marketplace into making money?

I generate money in multiple ways and my platform feeds them all.

- Book sales
- One-on-one clients and group coaching programs—aimed at both patients and my fellow visionaries
- Paid public speaking events
- Leading workshops and conferences
- Selling e-courses and other virtual content (mp3s, PDFs, video, teleseminars, and more)
- Corporate spokesperson gigs and sponsorships
- Using my platform to support my husband, who runs a business helping people achieve financial freedom; and by running a business with Dr. Christiane Northrup and her daughter Kate Northrup via Team Northrup (the multilevel marketing vitamin company USANA)

If you could back in time and do it all over again, what would you tell your younger self in terms of platform?

Oh, if only someone had told me to put a free opt-in in the upper right corner of OwningPink.com three years ago! After two years of great traffic, we had only 1,200 people on our newsletter list. (The sign-up was buried way down on the page and there was no free gift to entice people to fill it out.) The minute someone told me to offer a free gift, we got 5,000 new sign ups in a month! Free teleseminars and telesummits (I'm about to do my first) are another great way to grow your list quickly.

Is there anything else you would like to add about platform?

Stay true to your integrity. I can't tell you how many times I have said no, even though it sounded like such a good platform-building opportunity. Listen to your gut (which I call your "inner pilot light," that wise part of you that really knows what's best for you, your body, your relationships, and your business). Don't let fear rule the show.

In the beginning, I said yes to everything because I was afraid I'd miss an opportunity, and I wound up quickly burned out, depleted. But you can't lead or heal from a place of depletion. You must heal yourself first in order to change the world. That's the one lesson I'd share with aspiring authors/visionaries/healers. Don't let platform building spiral you downwards. Fill yourself first. Learn to say no. Create healthy boundaries. Raise your vibration. Attract others who share this vibration. Avoid the temptation to get sucked into doing everything for everybody. You are enough doing exactly what you're doing. Resist the urge to continually do *more*.

Brette Sember

NONFICTION—COOKING, LIFESTYLE, FINANCE, AND MORE

Brette Sember has written over thirty-five books in the last fourteen years. Here are a few: *The Parchment Paper Cookbook* (Adams Media, 2010), a book featuring healthy, easy meals in parchment paper packets with absolutely no pots and pans to clean up afterwards; *The Divorce Organizer & Planner* (McGraw-Hill, 2004), a guide to everything you need to get organized and work through your divorce; and *The Complete Credit Repair Kit* (3rd edition, Sourcebook, 2010), a guide to managing and improving your credit and financial life. Brette is a former attorney and lives with her husband, children, and dogs in western New York State. Her website is BretteSember.com.

When did you first start to stand out in your market?

I started writing books before *platform* was a dirty word, or even something anyone cared about. My early books built on top of each and, in essence, *became* my platform. When I decided I wanted to change direction and start writing about food, platform became key. I started my blog, MarthaAndMe. net, where I set off on a one-year journey to apprentice myself to Martha Stewart. In the back of my mind, a book was the goal, but I was also simply interested in the journey and blogging about food. This blog became popular because it was in the wake of the *Julie & Julia* craze, and also because I was completely honest about which recipes and projects worked and which didn't. Whenever I blogged a Martha recipe or project, I left a comment on the recipe or instructions on Martha's site, with a link to that blog entry. That brought me a lot of traffic. I also started commenting on other blogs that had to do with Martha and that brought me more traffic.

Somehow, the folks at MSLO [Martha Stewart Living Omnimedia] heard about me and I was invited to be a guest on *Morning Living Live*, the radio show on Martha's Sirius channel. I was invited back many, many times. My traffic was getting quite good on the blog.

Ultimately, I ended up not selling a book about this experience but continued the blog with a shift to include my own recipes and projects. From here, I decided to start a second blog, NoPotCooking.com, which focused on cooking in parchment paper. This time I was determined to sell a book. And I did within a few months. The Martha and Me blog showed publishers I could develop a following and blog on a continuous basis. No Pot Cooking simply showed them that my concept was a good one. So it was the two blogs together that got me the book deal.

Jumping forward to today, what do you consider the major aspects of your platform—the ones that are largest and most helpful in selling books and making money?

> I believe blogs are king. But I think you have to demonstrate dexterity with social media—get your Twitter numbers up and have a Facebook page related to your topic. I also believe that doing interviews and guest blogs is really important to extend your reach and grow your audience.

What opportunities have you had that have come through connections on social media?

> Lots. A company that makes parchment paper approached me via Twitter and we are going to work together. I've had lots of chances to guest blog or do interviews because of social media.

Billy Coffey

FICTION—INSPIRATIONAL

Billy Coffey is the author of three novels that all have Christian elements and themes: *Snow Day* (FaithWords, 2010), *Paper Angels* (FaithWords, 2011), and *Into the Maybe* (Thomas Nelson, 2012). He runs the popular blog, What I Learned Today (billycoffey.com/blog). He is a proud small-town Virginian, and lives with his wife and two children in the Shenandoah Valley.

When did you first start to stand out in your market?

My goal to get a book published came well before any thought of a platform. This was back in the late 1990s and early 2000s, when the Internet was still somewhat in its infancy. I had a publisher who was very interested in a manuscript I'd written but ultimately passed because, in their words, "Nobody knows who you are." Their advice was given in three words: *Start a blog*—easy enough in theory, but not so much in application. It took a long while to really develop an audience, but the experience paid off.

Jumping forward to today, what do you consider the major aspects of your platform—the ones that are largest and most help you sell books and make money?

Far and away, the major aspect of my platform is a professional website that contains a bio, information on the books I've written, contact information, and a blog. These days an author has to do more than simply write, he or she has to be accessible to others. I spend just as much time writing for my website and keeping its contents current as I do on my next novel.

What do you enjoy about platform building?

I've met some wonderful people through platform building, and that's been the most rewarding aspect. A small-town guy like me never thought I could form lasting friendships with people on the other side of the country, but that's exactly what's happened.

What do you dislike about it?

It takes an enormous amount of time, and very often that's time I have to carve out minute by minute through my day. I'm not fortunate enough to write full time. I have a job during the day and a family to care for. Often my novels get written late at night. In all that rush, things like getting on Twitter and writing a blog post can easily be put aside. It takes discipline to make sure you're doing the things you need to.

What opportunities have you had that have come through connections on social media?

In a somewhat roundabout way, my connections through social media resulted in signing with both my agent and my first publisher. I'd queried Rachelle Gardner about the manuscript that became my first book. She passed. But about a year later,

CREATE YOUR WRITER PLATFORM

one of her writers connected with me through Twitter and began reading my blog. She enjoyed it so much that she asked Rachelle to give me a second look. Thankfully, Rachelle did just that and became my agent a short time later.

When FaithWords expressed an interest in *Snow Day*, a big part of why they offered me a contract was that they'd spent some time around my website reading the comments to my blog posts. While some of my commenters have been reading my blog since its inception, the vast majority are people who come from Twitter and Facebook.

In your mind, what are you doing differently from others that leads to platform success?

Even though I'm a novelist, I wanted my blog posts to have little to do with fiction. I've found a majority of fiction writers use their blogs to either discuss the publishing industry or the craft of writing. Both approaches certainly have their merits, and many of these writers maintain strong followings. In my case I wanted to give readers an inside look at my own life. I wanted them to get to know the person behind the books—to invest in me and not just my words.

If you could go back in time and do it all over again, what would you tell your younger self in terms of platform?

I would have definitely started building my platform earlier. My younger self was stubborn and ignorant. I was one of those people who thought I could buck the system. I didn't need a platform. My words would speak for me. And yet everything I've been able to achieve to this point is the direct result of finally understanding the importance of platform.

What do you see as the future of your platform building?

My goal is to simply keep increasing my exposure. The bright spot is that it's never been easier. Thanks to the Internet and social media, the world is quite literally at our fingertips.

Is there anything else you would like to add?

It's obvious to any writer that the publishing industry is changing. The old rules and ways of doing things are being abandoned out of marketplace necessity. That can be (and in many cases is) a scary thing to writers and publishers alike, but the one constant is that there continues to be an appetite for a good story. Whether fair or not, getting your good story into the hands of the public now depends in large part upon your reach, and your reach depends in large part upon your savvy with blogs and social media. That can be a scary thing. Writers are notoriously withdrawn and even shy. The idea of having to "put yourself out there" can be tantamount to having to tap dance in front of a firing squad.

But it can be done. I promise that, and I offer myself as proof.

ſuſan Henderſon

FICTION

Susan Henderson is a two-time Pushcart Prize nominee and the recipient of an Academy of American Poets award. Her debut novel, *Up From the Blue*, was published by HarperCollins in 2010 and has been selected as a Great Group Reads pick by the Women's National Book Association, an outstanding softcover release by NPR, a Best Bets Pick by BookReporter, and a favorite reads feature on the *Rosie O'Donnell Show*. Susan blogs at LitPark.com.

When did you first start to stand out in your market?

> I started LitPark in 2006 as a reaction to my own frustration with writing and publishing—the bouts of self-doubt over manuscripts I could never seem to finish and rejection letters that felt debilitating. I not only brought my perspective as a writer but as a magazine editor who knew industry secrets, short-

cuts to publication, and the knowledge of what it's like to be the one doing the rejecting.

And so I started an open conversation—one I hoped would draw out others who were also feeling the great pull to write but a great aversion to being repeatedly punched in the gut. I named the site LitPark because I had a vision of a literary playground where writers could talk about the industry and their projects but in a way that renewed energy and confidence and the pure fun of writing.

I pulled readers from communities I was already involved in—Zoetrope, MySpace, and Publishers Marketplace—and posted about topics that had proven to be engaging. I not only responded to every comment but I thanked and linked each commenter at the end of the week as an incentive to join the conversation rather than just lurk.

Jumping forward to today, what do you consider the major aspects of your platform—the ones that are largest and most helpful in selling books and making money?

LitPark tapped into that inner battle between a writer's hunger to tell a story and the frustration with trying to get published. I was surprised by the strength of the community that formed, how word of mouth brought more and more strangers to the conversation. At first (and I've since scaled back), I offered a question of the week, an interview, and a weekly summary of insights I gained from the conversation, but it was the comment thread that burst alive. There we vented, celebrated, shared editing and publishing secrets, shared encouragement, and could see with some distance that what looks like failure is often part of the road to success.

What do you enjoy about platform building?

I love the sense of community, how the group sharing leads to new insights, creative sparks, and a sense of perspective on what it takes to stay in and succeed at this game. I have seen others pull out of depression and writer's block and get back in the game, find new ways around obstacles, and ultimately find success.

What do you dislike about it?

There's no question that the biggest problem with having a platform is that other writers, publicists, and publishers constantly ask you to use it to promote their work. My website already takes time I barely have, and I already consider it a community service—my way of giving back, of sharing what I know, of helping to buoy spirits. But sometimes dozens of times a month, I get requests for interviews, reviews, mentions, blurbs. It makes me feel used when people constantly ask for more than I can or want to give. For those of us whose greatest pleasure is reading, or who have particular topics we're trying to research or particular books we're dying to get to, it feels awful to have others place their books and their agenda on your reading list.

Look back at your road to writing success and try to identify the tipping points that influenced your platform.

My tipping point was when I did a feature with Neil Gaiman about the history of his hair. Before that interview, my traffic was pretty stable at ten thousand unique visitors a month, but afterwards the stats were thirty thousand and growing steadily. That post also got a mention in the *L.A. Times*, which brought more readers. Though the tipping point came overnight, there was a lot in place to support it. For one thing, I had created a reputation of being a good and unique interviewer, of never ever using an author's e-mail afterward, and of creating positive attention for anyone I featured. This allowed me to approach established authors to appear on LitPark. And once the visitors came to the site, they often stayed to look through the archives that were filled with interviews and lively conversations about the publishing world and the process of writing.

What opportunities have you had that have come through connections on social media?

One of the fastest-moving interactions I had on social media came after a friend of mine heard Rosie O'Donnell mention my book on her radio show. I found Rosie's Twitter handle and simply wrote, "Thank you @Rosie for mentioning my book!" She wrote back within about five seconds, "I love it. Want to be on my show?" It was amazing how quickly I had a team of publicists coordinating all the details, the very same people who rarely returned my e-mails.

Despite the great results from Twitter, that's not my social media of choice. The conversations feel disjointed to me, like millions of people shouting at the same time. I definitely prefer my own website and Facebook—both feel as if I'm inviting people into my living room, and we have one conversation at a time. Through these two venues, there have been so many opportunities: teaching gigs, interviews, anthologies, invitations to publisher parties. The greatest was a big blogger push when my book came out. About seventy-five book bloggers got together and planned a celebration launch, each telling their readers about my book as a way of thanking me for what I'd brought to the writer community. My publisher was very excited about the possibilities of a sales spike, but for me, it was just an overwhelming sense of heart—a realization that having those conversations and that outlet had mattered.

In your mind, what are you doing differently from others that leads to platform success?

I see my website as a community. I respond to every single comment and remember the stories of struggles and triumphs of everyone who posts there. That feels different to me than other sites where the emphasis is on the original post, and the importance of the poster, rather than on the reader and the conversations they drive in response to the post.

How do you translate your visibility in the marketplace into making money?

> It opens doors, all the time. I've been asked to be on panels, offered speaking engagements, and invited to book clubs. The speaking engagements and readings usually bring in about $1,000 per appearance. I do the book clubs and libraries for free because I think it's important to support them.

If you could go back in time and do it all over again, what would you tell your younger self in terms of platform?

> If I could do it again, I wish I'd found a way to keep people from sending me books to review in a way that doesn't feel personal—some kind of magical blanket statement, if there is such a thing. This would be the greatest gift I could give my family and my own writing life.

Amy Julia Becker

MEMOIR

Amy Julia Becker is the author of *A Good and Perfect Gift: Faith, Expectations and a Little Girl Named Penny* (Bethany House, 2011), named one of the Top Books of 2011 by *Publishers Weekly*, as well as *Penelope Ayers: A Memoir* (XLibris, 2008). A graduate of Princeton University and Princeton Theological Seminary, she blogs regularly for Patheos at Thin Places. Her essays have appeared in the *New York Times*, *First Things*, the *Philadelphia Inquirer*, the *Hartford Courant*, *The Christian Century*, *Christianity Today*, The Huffington Post, and Parents.com. Amy Julia lives with her husband, Peter, and three children in Lawrenceville, New Jersey.

When did you first start to stand out in your market?
> I wrote my first book, *Penelope Ayers*, without any awareness of the writing market. I tried to find an agent when I had no plat-

form or publishing experience, and I failed. At the same time, however, an agent who declined *Penelope Ayers* suggested that I work on a proposal for a memoir about our daughter Penny, who had been born with Down syndrome a few years earlier.

As I worked on the proposal, I wrote my first op-ed about prenatal testing and Down syndrome. It was published in the *Philadelphia Inquirer*. Otherwise, however, when my proposal went on the market, I still had very little publishing experience online or in print. Six editors expressed interest in the book, but all six declined because their marketing departments assumed they wouldn't be able to sell a book from an unknown author.

Although I was discouraged by the inability to find a publisher, I was encouraged by the idea that the writing and the story had appealed to editors. I decided it was time to build a platform. Technically speaking I had a blog at that point, but I was only posting once or twice a month. In the summer of 2009, I made a commitment (to myself) to blog at least two times each week. A slow but steady band of readers came next, with great encouragement from many of them to keep writing. Less than a year after that, I was invited to become a regular contributor to her.meneutics, the women's blog of *Christianity Today*. A few months later, beliefnet invited me to move my blog onto their site, an action which expanded my audience and my credibility. Simultaneously, two editors who had started reading my blog based upon my posts at her.meneutics, contacted me to see if I had any book ideas. Two months later (a year from the initial attempt), I had a contract with Bethany House to write *A Good and Perfect Gift*. My eventual success in finding a publisher came through a combination of quality writing and persistent blogging.

Jumping forward to today, what do you consider the major aspects of your platform—the ones that are largest and most helpful to selling books and making money?

My online presence is still the most significant aspect of my platform. I continue to blog regularly for patheos.com. I write for *Christianity Today*, and I contribute regularly to Lisa Belkin's parenting blog (now on The Huffington Post, formerly Motherlode of the *New York Times*). Consistent writing about the intersection of faith, family, and disability has led to interviews, guest posts, and opportunities to write longer articles in the case of *Christianity Today* and *The Christian Century*.

I have also become a well-known speaker on topics relating to faith, family, and disability. I've learned that I need to charge people when I speak. I used to think that I could sell enough books to cover the cost of travel, time, and preparation, but I rarely came close to breaking even. Because I have young kids at home, I only travel for speaking once a month at the most, but I have now developed a speaking policy which states clearly my need to be paid a stipend for whatever talk I give in addition to having my travel costs reimbursed. As a result, I feel less pressure to sell books, and I think I'm seen as a more legitimate speaker in my own right.

Finally, I've started to learn how to say no, both to writing and speaking opportunities. Because I have had some small success as a writer, I receive offers to review books and other products from a variety of sources. I'm learning how to stay focused on the topics that interest me most, and about which I have the most to say instead of jumping on every offer that comes my way.

What do you enjoy about platform building?

I enjoy the relational aspects. I am now a member of the Redbud Writers Guild, a group of Christian women writers. We have a Facebook group in which we share our written work and offer support to one another. I've formed similar relationships with writers through her.meneutics, Patheos, and with editors at Parents.com and Lisa Belkin of The Huffington Post. The relationships have become somewhat mutual, which is to say, I am able to not only offer my writing, but also to receive advice, encouragement, and critique from my writing friends and colleagues.

I've attended a few writers conferences as well as conferences related to Down syndrome in the past few years, and the relationships from those personal interactions have also led to wonderful opportunities and encouragement.

Finally, I enjoy blogging. It forces me to put some ideas into the public sphere every day, and I've grown considerably as a writer because of this discipline.

What do you dislike about it?

I dislike the relentlessness of it. A few months ago, I took a hiatus from daily blogging because it had begun to consume all my writing time, which meant I had very little opportunity to work on larger projects (or take care of myself and my family, for that matter). Ideally I would post something on my blog every day and then promote it via multiple pages on Facebook, Twitter, and Google+. Platform building is never done, and there are always many things I could do better. It takes an incredible amount of self-discipline to turn away from social media and work on other things.

Look back at your road to writing success and try to identify the tipping points that influenced your platform.

I'm not sure I've hit a tipping point yet, but I can identify a number of substantial boosts along the way. They all, by the way, come back to blogging. In one case, the editor of my college's alumni magazine contacted me after reading some of my blog posts. I wrote an essay in response, and Lisa Belkin, a fellow alumna, read the essay and reached out to me. One Mother-lode post led to a radio interview, another to an interview with Time.com. Later, HuffPo decided to promote my post on their own site as well as on AOL, and as a result it had ninety thousand views. None of these things in and of themselves tipped my book into bestseller status, but they all have helped me gain a voice within our culture, and they have certainly helped book sales.

I also saw a strong uptick in book sales as a result of receiving a starred review in *Publishers Weekly*. Later, the magazine named *A Good and Perfect Gift* one of the Top Ten Religion Books of 2011. This recognition underscores for me the relationship between spending time building a platform (social media, blogging, guest posts for other blogs) and spending time writing well.

In your mind, what are you doing differently from others that leads to platform success?

I don't play by all the "rules" of platform building, and I hope this ultimately enhances my platform rather than detracting from it. For the most part, I do less platform building—in the form of reading other blogs, commenting on other blogs, writing guest posts, and even posting on my own blog—than I "should." I probably should pay much more attention to SEO than I do. But given the time constraints of working part time with three small children, I've found that I need to be very disciplined about continuing to write substantive articles, essays, and ultimately books rather than letting platform building take over all of my work time. Of course, some bloggers maintain excellent quality and manage to blog regularly, speak, and write beautiful books. That's just not me.

Finally, I was told that I needed to post at least once every day, incorporate lots of images, and that each post should be 200 to 300 words. I've realized that the quality of my blog suffers tremendously if I try to live by those rules. To sum it up, I'd say I've become aware of the "best practices" of blogging and social media, but I've also allowed myself to work within my own boundaries.

How do you translate your visibility in the marketplace into making money?

For the most part, I am able to make money writing articles and book reviews on commission, and via speaking engagements. I hope that in time, good writing and a consistent presence will translate into book sales (and paychecks), but for now I'm content with writing about topics that interest me and matter to me.

If you could go back in time and do it all over again, what would you tell your younger self in terms of platform?

My greatest success has been my blog. I've wasted time speaking without pay, especially when there is travel involved. I've also wasted time (and money) creating a website. I need a website, but I should have been far more realistic about how much time it would take and what that time is worth.

In addition, I would have begun blogging and writing short essays from the start. Not only would I have gained readers (and perhaps a book contract) much earlier, but I also would have benefitted as a writer from blogging. Blogging has improved the quality of my writing, and it also gives me a place to try out ideas. Most days, I write something, and two or three people comment on it and a few dozen share it through social media. But every so often, I write something and it provokes dozens of comments and hundreds of shares. I pay attention to that type of reaction because it means I should possibly write more about the same topic.

Is there anything else you would like to add?

My biggest warning is that you can't do it all. I've tried to approach platform building like organic farming. I'm cultivating what grows (my audience, hopefully), but I'm trying to do so without gimmicks and with integrity and respect for the writing itself. I hope that this is a sustainable method that will also bear fruit, so to speak, with a faithful and steadily, if slowly, growing audience. I think a lot about limitations and possibilities. If I limit my time platform building, I open up time for family or exercise or working on a larger project. If I focus on the possibilities of platform building, I limit my time for those other things. I try to keep it all in balance rather than thinking that I can, or should, do it all.

ſarah PeKKanen

FICTION

Sarah Pekkanen is the internationally best-selling author of *The Opposite of Me*, *Skipping a Beat*, and *These Girls*, as well as the original linked short e-stories "All Is Bright" and "Love, Accidentally." Her novels have won rave reviews from *O Magazine*, *People*, *Harper's Bazaar*, and the *Washington Post*. A former journalist who has also worked as a waitress and photographic model, Sarah lives in Maryland with her family. Visit her website at sarahpekkanen.com.

When did you first start to stand out in your market?

A week before my first novel was published, everything changed for me. But first a little background: I'm a former journalist, and I research compulsively. And after selling *The Opposite of Me* to Atria Books, I began to learn as much as I could about the publishing industry—and then I started to panic. I quickly learned that the vast majority of books fail to earn back their advances, and that low initial sales can affect the rest of an author's career. I've wanted to write books since I was a kid, and I finally had a chance at my dream job. Now I was learning that the odds were stacked against my keeping that job.

So I decided to do everything I possibly could to be in that small percentage of authors who earn out their advances and actually make their publishers money. Very soon after signing a contract, I decided to spend my entire United States advance for *Opposite* on marketing and publicity. I hired a freelance publicist a year before my novel hit stores, and kept her on my payroll for four months after publication. I hired a terrific web designer to create a professional landing place for readers trying to find out more about me. I took out thousands of dollars in blog ads. I made up postcards featuring my book cover and gave them out whenever possible. I set up Facebook and Twitter accounts. I took out Facebook ads. I set up book signings.

Still, I felt like it wasn't enough. I knew the elusive, shimmering phenomenon called "going viral" was what every author, artist, and businessperson dreamed of—and I was no exception. Then one of my friends (a very savvy writer) suggested I try to drive pre-sales a week before my publication day. Her reasoning was that a spike in Amazon sales would cause Amazon to recommend my book more frequently, and early sales would also make booksellers take notice and perhaps prompt them to order *The Opposite of Me* for their stores. It would give my book a running start. I liked the idea of people preordering my book, but I hated the idea of asking them to do so. So I decided to make it fun—I'd gather some great prizes and hold a raffle. Anyone who preordered my book on "Sarah Spike Day," as we called it, got an entry to win an e-reader, a basket of books, a shipment of Godiva chocolates, and various other goodies.

Then the unexpected happened: the well-known author Jennifer Weiner heard about my plan through our mutual editor. Jennifer was one of the first authors to plunge into social media, and she was intrigued. She also tries to help new authors—and so she decided to help me in a big way. She added to my Sarah Spike Day prizes by donating a signed copy of any one of her bestselling books to every single person who pre-ordered mine. So for the price of my book, everyone also got a signed Jennifer Weiner book—as well as a shot at a raffle prize.

It was breathtaking. The day before Spike Day, my Amazon ranking was about 250,000. By the end of spike day, it was #68 and at Barnes & Noble, we broke the top 30. *The Opposite of Me* went into a second printing before it was even published.

Jumping forward to today, what do you consider the major aspects of your platform—the ones that are largest and most help you sell books and make money?

Facebook and Twitter are huge—I'm there almost every day, interacting with readers. I also hire a publicist for every novel.

It might sound odd, but I try to think of myself as being the Nordstrom of authors. I view my books as a small business, and I know that a solid foundation will give them the best potential for growth. I was inspired by the founder of Honest Tea [a bottled organic tea company] while researching my second novel, *Skipping a Beat*. I met with the founder because I wanted to model my character's business after Honest Tea—but I also learned a lot about investing early in your own business and working like crazy to make it a success. So I try to be as involved as I can in every aspect of my novels—from securing cover quotes to coming up with unusual ideas to keep them selling.

I value creativity, both in my novels and in my approach to platform. When I see a lot of people doing the same thing—like Facebook contests, which I believe are overdone—I try to look for something different. For example, I write a humor column for my local city magazine. I'm in negotiations over my fee for this, as it's time for a raise. Yesterday, I e-mailed the editor to say I was willing to accept a lower rate if he would give me a free, one-page ad for my books this spring, when my third novel will be published. I'm waiting to hear back from him on that. If it doesn't work out, I'll come up with another plan.

Being respectful to readers and bloggers is very important to me, both personally and professionally. Not everyone is going to love your book—so don't make a scene and write them a nasty e-mail or blast them on social media when this inevitably happens. I take the opposite approach: If someone on Goodreads mentions that they didn't like my book, and I come across that review, I send them a note letting them know I'm sorry that particular book wasn't right for them, but I hope they give my other books a chance. When bloggers review my book, I thank them for taking the time to do so. I answer every letter or e-mail personally. Readers like connecting with authors, and they become loyal when a relationship is established. And it's certainly a two-way street. When I'm feeling isolated or stressed or insecure, I pop over to Facebook and bask in the kind words of my readers. The relationship is very real, even though I've never met some of these folks. I enjoy and appreciate them.

I also take every opportunity to pick the brains of folks who seemed to know a lot about social media. I remember one dinner party I attended when I found myself sitting next to a guy who worked at an Apple Store and knew a lot about social media. You can bet I monopolized that poor man all night long, peppering him with questions. Just the other day, I watched Justin Bieber's documentary—not because I'm a fan but because I heard he leveraged social media in a huge way before becoming a star. I wanted to see how he did it.

What do you enjoy about platform building?

I absolutely adore interacting with readers on Facebook and Twitter. It's one of the first places I go when I have good news, and readers and bloggers are wonderful and very generous about sharing the excitement with me. I also like trying new things and seeing what resonates in terms of additional sales or additional fans. It's a terrific challenge. Publishing is one of business's most complex puzzles. No one knows why a book that's given a $1 million advance and glowing reviews can tank—while a little novel that was sold for a few thousand bucks suddenly soars and becomes a breakout bestseller. I'm fascinated by this—and I'm constantly learning as much as I can about the publishing industry, from every possible angle. It's a frustrating, beautiful, compelling mystery.

What do you dislike about it?

Asking other authors for favors like cover quotes. I know how busy writers are, and I cringe when I reach out and ask someone I really admire to take a chunk of time out of their day to do me a favor. But I do it when I need to, and I try to pay it back by helping other authors when they need a hand.

There's nothing else I hate about it, but I have learned that some things are more effective than others. For example, I set up lots of book signings for my first novel. It wasn't the smartest move. (After all, when was the last time you went to a book signing for an author you didn't know, who wasn't a household name?) Although I love meeting bookstore owners and signing stock, it would've been smarter to stop by, shake hands, and move on, rather than sitting at a table for two hours casting bright and somewhat desperate smiles at all the folks who were trying to sneak by me and pick up the new John Grisham novel.

Look back at your road to writing success and try to identify the tipping points that influenced your platform.

Sarah Spike Day was my biggest tipping point. Not only did I get hundreds of new Facebook and Twitter friends overnight because folks wanted to know more about the new author that Jen Weiner recommended, but I also wrote a back-page article for *Publishers Weekly* about the experience, which made my name known to many people in the industry. And while I agree tipping points are wonderful, there's also something to be said for the slow, steady, relentless build. I'm putting my efforts into both.

What opportunities have you had that have come through connections on social media?

Being friendly and genuine on social media has led to lots of opportunities. For example, the author Jen Lancaster and I met via social media—and we later blurbed each other's books and have become good friends. We support each other professionally and personally, which is something authors need in this field. I've never subscribed to the theory that readers are like a pie, and if one author takes a big slice of them, there will be less for the rest of us. I think the opposite is true: When readers hear authors promote one another and get genuinely excited about books, they're inspired to read even more.

In your mind, what are you doing differently from others that leads to platform success?

Some people that I talk to seem to think there's a secret to building a platform—say, if you just get reviewed by these five blogs, then your book is going to explode. And I wondered, too, if there was a secret system I didn't know about when I first started out. But now I don't think it really works that way. I think consistency is the key, and that's one thing I'm committed to. Consistency, and sincerity. If you hate being on Facebook, people will be able to tell. Readers are perceptive. They also know when you're just trying to push them to buy your book, and they recoil from it—and rightly so. Your platform needs to mesh with your personality.

What do you see as the future of your platform building?

First, to write the best books I possibly can. There's no more effective way to build platform than through the word of mouth of readers. They're the ones with the real power in this industry, and that's just as it should be. As for plans and goals, I'll continue to seek out new and creative ways to market my novels. I can't say what those things are now, because the landscape is fluid and ever changing. A few years ago, I wasn't on Facebook. Now I can't go two days without checking in there. Who knows what the next five years will bring? But I know what I'll bring—an open mind, a zeal to explore new opportunities, and a constant commitment to building my books.

Christelyn Karazin

NONFICTION—SELF-HELP/RELATIONSHIPS

Christelyn Denise Karazin is a health, lifestyle, business, and education writer for such high-profile publications as *Woman's Day, Better Homes & Gardens, Ebony, Pregnancy Magazine,* Reuters News Service, and many more. Her book, *Swirling: How to Date, Mate and Relate, Mixing Race, Culture, and Creed,* was released in 2012 by Simon & Schuster. Prior to magazine writing, she was a public relations professional who specialized in consumer and legal public relations, and represented such clients as Jenny McCarthy and Dr. Jay Gordon in their co-project regarding vaccinations, resulting in a prime placement on *Larry King Live.* She earned her Bachelor of Arts degree in communications, cum laude, from Loyola Marymount University in Los Angeles.

When did you first start to stand out in your market?

> I started platform building sort of backwards. I got the book deal, and then my agent suggested I start a blog, because, frankly, no one knew who I was! The blog, Beyond Black & White, was at first just going to be an outlet for me while I wrote my book. I would chronicle what I'd discovered in my research and interviews, and perhaps provide an opportunity to gain sources. I had no idea the popularity of the blog would explode.

Jumping forward to today, what do you consider the major aspects of your platform—the ones that are largest and most helpful in selling books and making money?

> I think what's working for me is that I use multiple forms of social media to gain awareness about the blog and the book. Facebook is a big one, but I also use Google+, Twitter, and YouTube. I think it's important to have a multimedia approach to exposing yourself. Don't just blog. Podcast. Produce videos. Stand on your head. (Just kidding about that last one. Kinda.)

What do you enjoy about platform building?

> Honestly, it's like watching a child grow. You put all your blood, sweat, and tears into it, and then, when you see the outcome of all that effort, your chest can't help but puff out a bit. Platform building has also given me unprecedented access to a network of sources, experts, colleagues, and friends. And because I do this from the comfort of a home office, showering is optional.

Look back at your road to writing success and try to identify the tipping points that influenced your platform.

> That's easy. I created an online protest—the first of it's kind—to address the 73 percent out-of-wedlock rate in the African-American community called, "No Wedding No Womb." I rallied over one hundred bloggers to write on the same day, about the same thing, but in their own words. It went viral. It was tweeted

over 100,000 times in one night. We got international press coverage, including the Associated Press.

In your mind, what are you doing differently from others that leads to platform success?

I think something that I'm doing that you don't see much is that I don't mind sharing the spotlight, and I like giving others an opportunity to shine. I welcome guest posters, I promote other people's ventures, I feature regular people doing notable things. I also run my blog like an online magazine and even have an editorial staff. I think having a diversity of voices adds to the flavor and interest of the medium.

How do you translate your visibility in the marketplace into making money?

I monetize my blog through Google ads, my own ad accounts in which I've secured, and through an affiliate program called BlogHer. I have a page and category dedicated to promoting the book, too, of course.

Final Thoughts

Creating a writer platform is an intensely difficult yet incredibly valuable endeavor. When you do it, you're taking the reins of your own journey, and more specifically, of your own writing destiny. You understand that writers today must be more than writers, and the goal is not to fight change but rather to make change work for you. If you made your way through this entire book and are starting to implement the instruction, I have some good news to share: You are ahead of the pack. You understand how success is created, and you're on the road to your final goal. I congratulate you and wish you well.

If you feel overwhelmed by the amount of advice and information in this book, don't be. Just take your journey day by day—but resolve to make each day *count*. Always be moving forward. Always be creating something or connecting with someone. My hope is that this book has not overwhelmed you but, rather, *motivated* you.

If I achieved my goals and if all the other authors who chimed in achieved their goals as well, then why not you, too? From everything I've learned about writing, accomplishing what you wish only requires two things: passion and time dedicated to your cause. My challenge to you is to give up that which you like in pursuit of that which you love.

To conclude, I just want to say thank you for reading my book. I welcome your feedback and communication; find me on Twitter

@chucksambuchino, search me on Facebook, or just stop by my author website (chucksambuchino.com). I hope to see you at a writers conference or connect with you online soon. Good luck!

ABOUT THE AUTHOR

CHUCK SAMBUCHINO (chucksambuchino.com) is the editor of *Guide to Literary Agents* as well as *Children's Writer's & Illustrator's Market* (both Writer's Digest Books). He is the author of the writing guide *Formatting & Submitting Your Manuscript*, 3rd ed. (2009) and runs the Guide to Literary Agents Blog (guidetoliteraryagents.com/blog), one of the biggest blogs in publishing.

Chuck is also a humor book author. The film rights of his 2010 book, *How to Survive a Garden Gnome Attack*, were optioned by Sony. His latest humor book is *Red Dog / Blue Dog* (2012; reddog-bluedog.com), which pairs pooches and politics. Besides that, he is a husband, cover band guitarist, freelance editor, chocolate chip cookie addict, and owner of a flabby-yet-lovable dog named Graham. Connect with Chuck on Facebook or Twitter: @chucksambuchino.

INDEX